EVOLUTION IN RELIGION

EVOLUTION IN RELIGION

*A Study in Sri Aurobindo
and
Pierre Teilhard de Chardin*

BY

R. C. ZAEHNER

CLARENDON PRESS · OXFORD

1971

Oxford University Press, Ely House, London W.1

GLASGOW NEW YORK TORONTO MELBOURNE WELLINGTON
CAPE TOWN SALISBURY IBADAN NAIROBI LUSAKA ADDIS ABABA
DAR ES SALAAM BOMBAY CALCUTTA MADRAS KARACHI LAHORE
DACCA KUALA LUMPUR SINGAPORE HONG KONG TOKYO

PRINTED AND BOUND IN GREAT BRITAIN BY
HAZELL WATSON AND VINEY LTD
AYLESBURY BUCKS

For Satish and Alice Sircar

PREFACE

THE first three chapters of this book were delivered as lectures at St. Stephen's College, Delhi. They were the Westcott Lectures under the Teape Foundation for the year 1969. Under the Teape Foundation it is permissible to repeat these lectures at Bishop's College, Calcutta, and Christian College, Tamburam, Madras. I availed myself of this permissive clause and also of a kind invitation from Professor T. M. P. Mahadevan of Madras University to deliver an extra lecture to the Faculty of Philosophy there. This lecture appears as chapter IV in this book. The lecture was intended to be self-contained but also to fit in with the general theme of the Westcott Lectures. Hence the reader may find that the themes treated in the first three chapters are to some degree repeated in the fourth. It is to be hoped that these repetitions are not too obvious or too irksome.

In Delhi I had the extreme good fortune of being the guest of Principal Sircar and his wholly delightful wife at St. Stephen's College. To say that they spoiled me would be to put it mildly. They treated me with a parental kindness usually reserved for the proverbial child of six, which, in view of what Jesus of Nazareth says of little children, I take as the highest compliment one Christian can pay to another, and which is the way I like being treated anyhow. Not only did the Principal ensure that I should see all the sights of Delhi but he drove me there himself. He also bought me a ticket on the Taj Mahal express which leaves at 7.00 a.m. and ordered a taxi to get me there in good time. At the last moment, however, he relented since he considered (rightly) that I was far too stupid to be let loose in an Indian railway-station and therefore drove me there himself, thereby ensuring that I should get on the right train. He also laid on a most charming and efficient guide who was an alumnus of St.

Stephen's at the other end. In short there is nothing that he would not have done for me.

And what am I to say of his wife, Alice? First I must say that she is a superb cook and I doubt whether there was any Indian delicacy she did not prepare for me or any fruit she did not ensure that I tasted. Everything she offered me was delicious, but the gifts, I felt all the time I was there, were as nothing compared to the spirit in which they were given. Secondly I must record that Mrs. Sircar (like her husband) is quite one of the most delightful human beings I have met, and thirdly that, despite her charm, she is not the kind of person to put up with any nonsense.

After visiting Madras, Calcutta, and Banaras I again had the privilege of staying with the Sircars over Christmas, and on Christmas Day I was taken along to a lunch with some of the Naga community at which many St. Stephen's boys and old boys were present. Without the Naga contingent, I was told, the St. Stephen's football team could scarcely have achieved its present excellence. I quite believe it, for these Naga lads combine charm, gaiety, and perfect manners with an undeniable toughness. Nor shall I readily forget a young boy who, without revealing his name, told me after my second lecture that I should be a poet, not a lecturer, and asked for my blessing after the third. It is incidents like this that make India the lovable land it is.

Again I wish to thank Principal A. P. Thomson, his wife, and their staff for their most kind hospitality at Bishop's College, Calcutta, and Principal C. D. S. Devanesan, *his* wife, and their staff for theirs at Christian College, Tamburam. The list of other friends including, of course, a high sprinkling of Jesuits, is too long for me to mention all by name. I would, however, like to make special mention of Sri Deepankar Chatterjee of the Sri Aurobindo Centre in Calcutta who, out of the sheer goodness of his heart, gave me a bouquet of flowers and the *Spiritual Unfoldment* of Swami Abhedananda. I hope he will not take it amiss if I say that he seemed to radiate a luminous spirituality which was very real to me. May God bless him and all the friends I met in India.

And then I should mention Antony Wynn and Julian Baldick who made the checking of quotations almost enjoyable. I thank them too.

Lastly I would like to thank Éditions du Seuil of Paris for their kind permission to include extracts from the works of Teilhard de Chardin in a translation of my own which differs somewhat from the English versions published by Messrs Collins, and also Messrs Collins for concurring in this permission. And, having said that, I would add that when my anonymous young friend said I should have been a poet, he was really speaking of Teilhard, not of myself.

All Souls College,   R. C. Z.
Oxford
7 July 1970

CONTENTS

I

RELIGIONS AND RELIGION

'RELIGIOUS distress is at the same time the expression of real distress and the protest against real distress. Religion is the sigh of the oppressed creature, the heart of a heartless world, just as it is the spirit of a spiritless situation.'[1] This is a quotation and, you may be surprised to hear, it is from Marx. The next words are more familiar: they are, 'It is the opium of the people.'

What Marx meant was that so long as there was real distress and so long as the majority of mankind was oppressed by the minority, then it was the function of religion to appear as 'the heart of a heartless world' and 'the spirit of a spiritless situation': even so, in reality it was no more than 'the opium of the people'. Religion itself was but the ideological reflexion of a political reality. If, since the Enlightenment, religion had been more or less permanently under fire, this could only be followed by a more realistic attack on the social and political institutions which supported religion and, through their oppression of the majority—the proletariat—made religion necessary. Once the attack had been switched from the ideal enemy and concentrated on the real one, once the offensive had been switched from religion to politics, religion would itself automatically disappear. 'Thus,' Marx went on to say, 'the criticism of heaven turns into the criticism of the earth, the *criticism of religion* into the *criticism of right*, and the *criticism of theology* into the *criticism of politics*.'

This view came to be held by all 'progressives' in the latter half of the nineteenth century and is still gaining ground to-day. The secular age is in full swing in the once Christian

[1] K. Marx and F. Engels, *On Religion*, Moscow, Foreign Languages Publishing House, 1957, p. 42.

West and it is probably only a question of time before it will be in full swing in India as well as throughout the Muslim world. The intelligentsia is still overwhelmingly secularist, humanist, or agnostic; and organized religion is no longer taken seriously even among professing Christians, Buddhists, and Hindus.

In Europe the process of secularization started with the Renaissance and, whether the Reformers liked it or not, was immensely strengthened by the Reformation; for though the Papacy had always been mixed up in politics, it maintained nonetheless that it was superior to politics and therefore to all secular power. Though it had all too often been forced to do the will of secular princes, it never gave up its claim that its mission was above and beyond politics. Thus, as Marx again pointed out, 'When in the Holy Alliance at first a quasi-religious alliance of states was to be formed and religion was to be the state motto of Europe, *the Pope* showed profound sense and perfect consistency in refusing to join it, for in his view the universal Christian link between nations was the Church and not diplomacy, not a worldly alliance of states.' For 'the truly religious state is the theocratic state; the prince of such states must be either the God of religion, Jehovah himself, as in the Jewish state, God's representative, the Dalai Lama, as in Tibet, or finally . . . they must all submit to a Church which is an "infallible church". For if, as in Protestantism, there is no supreme head of the church, the domination of religion is nothing but the religion of domination, the cult of the will of the government.'[2]

This was the price that the Lutherans and Anglicans had to pay for identifying themselves with the secular power; and this too is the price that the Anglicans and (less justifiably) the Non-Conformist missions had to pay in India, for they too became identified with British imperial domination.

Marx was right: religion is not simply a matter for the individual. This is quite a modern idea, being the natural corollary of the proliferation of the Protestant sects which

[2] Ibid., pp. 35–6.

occurred and indeed was bound to occur once the visible unity of the Church had been shattered. But this was not all that the Protestants shattered; for, parallel and supplementary to the unity of the Church, ran a rich stream of contemplative wisdom culminating in the writings of St. John of the Cross and St. Teresa of Avila. This was, if you like, the inward dimension of which Catholic universality was the outward and complementary manifestation. For what, after all, does mysticism teach us? Broadly speaking it teaches us that all things are one in God who is the Centre on to which all other 'centres' converge. This is not just a Christian interpretation of an experience which, as all agree, is ineffable: we find it in such unaligned authors as Rousseau, Balzac, and Teilhard de Chardin; and we find it in the Upanishads, the Gītā, Rāmānuja, and Sri Aurobindo. Its earliest formulation, perhaps, is this from the *Brihadānyaka* Upanishad (2. 5. 15):

Just as the spokes of a wheel are fixed together on to the hub and felly, so are all contingent beings, all gods, all worlds, all vital breaths and all these selves fixed together in this Self.

Let no one think that I regard all mystical experiences as being ultimately the same. All that I have written shows that I do not; and I have not changed my mind. Nor should I now be lecturing on Aurobindo and Teilhard de Chardin if I had. All I would say now is that the convergence of human personalities on to the hub and felly of a divine centre is one of the main themes of mystical experience, and it is the one consistently emphasized by both Aurobindo and Teilhard who are between them the excuse and the main theme of these lectures.

The reason I have chosen them is that, in their separate traditions, they represent something totally new in mystical religion. And the reason is not far to seek. Both not only accepted the theory of evolution but enthusiastically acclaimed it, indeed were almost obsessed by it. Both were, it seems, profoundly influenced by Bergson, both were deeply dissatisfied with organized religion, and both were vitally concerned not only with individual salvation or 'liberation' but also with the *collective* salvation of mankind. Hence their sympathetic interest in Marxian socialism, for it was the hope of each of them that the unity in diversity which the mystic finds in himself would be reflected in a socialized and free society in which, as Marx had prophesied, 'we shall have an association in which the free development of each is the condition for the free development of all'[3].

The reality, as we know, has turned out to be very different from the prophecy both in the Soviet Union and in China. But need it have been so? 'It is not,' Aurobindo had written, 'that the principle of Communism necessitates any such results or that its system must lead to a termite civilization or the suppression of the individual; it could well be, on the contrary, a means at once of the fulfilment of the individual and the perfect harmony of a collective being. The already developed systems which go by the name are not really Communism but constructions of an inordinately rigid State Socialism.'[4]

All this could be: and indeed it was—for eight brief months of truly Communist faith, hope, and charity in Czechoslovakia in 1968. The shameful and essentially un-Marxist and anti-Marxist result we all know. Yet the seed has been sown, and are we being just starry-eyed and simple if we think the seed will one day bear fruit? If we *think* so, I am afraid we are, for Satan—that terrifying reality which has the insidious power to corrupt and poison every ideal—Satan is still prince of this world; and evolution, like the Holy Spirit which is perhaps the Spirit of evolution itself, is never in a hurry for it has all eternity in which to work out its mysterious purposes. However, there is always room for hope, and hope is a Christian virtue. It was also recognized as a virtue by Aurobindo though it seems to have faded from his vision towards the end of his life. For Aurobindo, though he had

---

[3] Marx and Engels, *The Communist Manifesto*, II end.

[4] Sri Aurobindo, *The Ideal of Human Unity* in *The Human Cycle* etc, Pondicherry, 1962, p. 795.

started off as a left-wing politician, had also been the subject
of a mystical revelation, and this even so Anglicized a Bengali
as Aurobindo could not lightly brush aside. On the contrary,
it stamped him indelibly with what he could not help accepting as its authenticity and truth. Moreover, he could not help
feeling that there must be some connexion between the collective Socialist ideal of unity in diversity and his own inner
experience of much the same thing. 'Cosmic consciousness',
as he called it following R. M. Bucke, in which the ego is
annihilated and all is seen as One and One as all in a perfect
and marvellous harmony, is the 'Truth' which the mystic
experiences in his own being; it must therefore be true of the
cosmos as a whole. Hence evil must either be illusory or a
necessary stepping-stone on the way to the good. This is the
common experience of all so-called 'nature mystics', and it
also has the scriptural authority of the Upanishads. For the
mystic the Absolute transcends all opposites; and it must
therefore transcend good and evil too, fusing and uniting
them in a higher synthesis. Mysticism is not concerned with
morality, certainly not with the 'negative' morality of 'thou
shalt not' which Aurobindo identified with the Semitic religions. Like the English medieval mystic, Julian of Norwich,
who declared on the authority of Jesus himself that 'It be-
hoveth that there should be sin; but all shall be well, and all
shall be well, and all manner of thing shall be well,'[5] so too
Aurobindo was to say: 'In God's providence there is no evil,
but only good or its preparation.'[6] Sayings like these can be
found in the writings of mystics of all religions and of none.
Hence mysticism has always been anathema to orthodox
Protestants and not least to the early Protestant missionaries
to India who could see nothing but evil in such sentiments as
these which they found richly represented in the indigenous
religion; for Hinduism, as I have said elsewhere[7], 'is the

[5] Julian of Norwich, *Revelations of Divine Love*, ch. 27.
[6] Aurobindo, *Thoughts and Aphorisms*, Pondicherry, 1958, p. 31.
[7] R. C. Zaehner, *Hindu and Muslim Mysticism*, London, Athlone Press, 1960,
p. 3.

E.R.—2

high-school of mysticism'. It is mystical to the core and only
peripherally concerned with morality as understood by the
moralists. For, as R. M. Bucke, himself no mystic by training,
said (he was in fact the son of a clergyman but himself a
'matter-of-fact scientist' who ended his career as the President
of the American Medico-Psychological Association), cosmic
'consciousness shows the cosmos to consist not of dead matter
governed by unconscious, rigid, and unintending law; it
shows it on the contrary as entirely immaterial, entirely
spiritual and entirely alive; it shows that death is an absurdity, that everyone and everything has eternal life; it shows
that the universe is God and that God is the universe, and
that no evil ever did or ever will enter into it.'[8] All this he
deduced from one mystical experience he had had and, like
so many nature mystics, he was so overpowered by the reality
of what he had experienced that he not only dismissed
organized religion as he knew it as so much make-believe but
also convinced himself that his own experience must be
typical of, if not identical with, all mystical experience. In
this he was rather naive. Aurobindo was less so, for he too had
experienced the omnipresence of God 'in every man moving
before me, even in every tree, wall, bird, and beast. . . . God
is in every metal, and in the earth and mud'[9] But he did not
suppose that this one experience was in itself either typical or
complete, although he is not always consistent about this. It
did, however, lead him to believe that in eternity where there
is neither space nor time evil can have no place. Maybe he
was right, and this is one of the questions we shall have to
consider later.

Teilhard de Chardin too was a pantheist by nature, and
throughout the first World War, during which he acted as a
stretcher-bearer, he seems to have lived in an almost permanent state of 'cosmic consciousness'. It was not he who had
sought it out any more than had Bucke. 'It was not I,' he

[8] R. M. Bucke, *Cosmic Consciousness*, New York, E. P. Dutton, 23rd ed., 1966,
p. 17.
[9] A. B. Purani, *Life of Sri Aurobindo*, Pondicherry, 1964, p. 125.

writes, 'who laboriously discovered the All; it was the All which showed itself to me, imposed itself on me through a kind of "cosmic consciousness". It is the attraction of the All that has set everything in motion in me, brought it to life and given it organic form. . . . [Hence] I can never aspire to a reward which is less than the All itself.'[10] And this cosmic consciousness, if it is to be truly cosmic, must be realized not only in individual men but also in the whole of mankind. Only so can humanity be spiritually unified and collectively redeemed.

Aurobindo and Teilhard de Chardin had these two things in common, the repeated experience of cosmic consciousness and a profound belief in evolution, the goal of which they saw to be the divinization of man. Both produced their most significant work during and directly after the first World War. Teilhard was prevented by his superiors from publishing anything during his lifetime; hence it would have been impossible for Aurobindo to have become conversant with his thought. It is, however, strange that Teilhard never came to hear of Aurobindo—or perhaps not so strange, for though he had formed his own ideas about Eastern mysticism, he had quite clearly not read even the basic texts in any kind of depth. Had he done so, he would scarcely have dismissed Eastern mysticism out of hand as being *périmé*, 'dated'[11], how much less Aurobindo whose thought so closely resembled his own. For what was the ideal of both men? 'The hope of the kingdom of heaven within us and the city of God upon earth'[12], as Aurobindo said, or, in the words of Teilhard, 'to promote in equal measure the mastery of the world and the kingdom of God'[13]. The two should go hand in hand; for man is, according to the mystics, a microcosm, an exact rep-

---

[10] Pierre Teilhard de Chardin, *Oeuvres* (Paris, Éditions du Seuil) 9, p. 72: cf. E.T. *Science and Christ*, London, 1968, pp. 43–44. (E.T. = English Translation, all the volumes of which are published by Messrs Collins.)

[11] *Oeuvres* 7, p. 236.

[12] Aurobindo, *The Human Cycle* etc., ch. 13, p. 165.

[13] *Écrits du temps de la guerre*, Paris, Grasset, 1965, p. 84: E.T. *Writings in Time of War*, 1968, p. 91.

lica *in parvo* of the universe as macrocosm. If, then, man can
realize the perfect harmony, the unity in diversity, of all
things centred upon himself, must it not follow that this
harmony is also the rule of the macrocosm too? Empirical
fact, however, contradicts this, and contradicts it violently.
And so Aurobindo was honest enough to say: 'Heaven we
have possessed, but not the earth; but the fullness of the Yoga
is to make . . . Heaven and earth equal and one.'[14] Or again,
'All is always for the best, but it is sometimes from the external point of view an awkward best.'[15] This is because what
the mystic experiences in cosmic consciousness transcends
time—he sees all things in one all-comprehensive sweep, in
eternity, as God sees them. This is the *waḥdat ash-shuhūd*, the
'unity of vision' of the Indian Muslim mystic Sirhindī as opposed to the *waḥdat al-wujūd*, the 'ontological unity' of Ibn
'Arabī and Śankara. From *this* point of view 'all *is* always for
the best', but from our own empirical point of view we can
say no more than 'all *shall* be well, all *shall* be well, and all
manner of thing *shall* be well.'

The great defect of mysticism is that it tends to by-pass the
problem of evil either by writing it off as illusory or at most an
appearance, as with Śankara, or by subsuming it and 'negat-
ing' it into that all-comprehensiveness which cosmic consciousness reveals. Conventional religion, particularly in the
Semitic tradition from which Christianity and Islam spring,
takes evil very seriously indeed: the mystic, and particularly
the Hindu mystic, on the other hand, tends to speak of *transcending* good and evil, for they are merely a pair of opposites
imposed by the discursive intellect on to a fundamental unity
where all the opposites coalesce and are reconciled.

Both Aurobindo and Teilhard de Chardin were mystics,
and mystics are of their very nature concerned with eternity
rather than with time; but they were also fervid believers in
evolution, and evolution can only take place within time. For
both the mystic and the evolutionist, however, the great
orthodoxies of the world are at the best approximations to the

[14] A. B. Purani, op. cit., p. 167.   [15] Ibid., p. 166.

truth or simply a stage in the evolutionary process which must be transcended and discarded in a supposedly rational and scientific age.

Teilhard de Chardin was profoundly dissatisfied with what he considered to be the excessive legalism of the Roman Catholic Church of his time. He was, however, a Jesuit, and it was the intention of the founder of his Order that it should be a *corps d'élite* in the personal service of the Pope, bound to him in corpse-like obedience. At every stage of his life his ideas and writings were suppressed not only by his own superiors but also by the curial authorities in Rome. Yet despite occasional bitterness it never seriously occurred to him to leave the Society of Jesus, let alone the Roman Church, for despite all its defects it was for him the only possible centre of unity in the frame of which the collective salvation of mankind could one day be realized. Despite its pettyfogging legalism and a sacramental system that had so often degenerated into an almost mechanical device by which salvation might be obtained, the Roman Church with the supreme Pontiff as Vicar of Christ at its head was still the only possible focus of unity which, acting as the axis of evolution itself, could mould mankind together into a unified and forward-thrusting collectivity destined ultimately to converge upon God as its true and predestined Centre.

Christianity [he said] now appears to me much less a closed and established whole than an axis of progression and assimilation. Apart from this axis, I cannot see any guarantee or any way out for the world. But around this axis, I can glimpse an immense quantity of truths and attitudes for which orthodoxy has not yet made room. If I dared use a word which could be given unacceptable meanings, I feel myself irreducibly 'hyper-Catholic.[16]

For Aurobindo the problem was quite different. Though born in Calcutta he was sent to England when he was seven. Educated at St. Paul's School in London and King's College, Cambridge, proving himself to be a classical scholar of note,

[16] Teilhard, (E.T.) *Letters to Léontine Zanta*, 1969, p. 36.

he was thoroughly steeped in the classical humanism of his time: by upbringing he was an English gentleman. This, however, did not prevent him from becoming interested in Socialism, an interest that he was never wholly to lose, since he saw in Socialism a more just society in which association would supplant competition and in which the individual ego, for him always the root of all evil and all ignorance, must be subordinated to the community. It was only on his return to India, however, that he discovered the Hindu religion and the Vedānta. But he could not accept the Vedānta in its classic non-dualist formulation, for in England he had come to accept Darwinism and Bergson's idea of *creative* evolution. If the One were totally static and unfractionable, as Śankara taught, then there could be no room for evolution, creativity, or development of any kind. This could not be. Rather, the One though absolutely sufficient unto itself, must also be the source of multiplicity and not only of change but of progressive, evolutionary change, an ascent the culmination of which was to be re-united with the One in a new richness and a new glory. Aurobindo knew that his 'integral Yoga' which not only aimed at the discovery of the immortal and timeless within oneself but also sought to harmonize the total human being in and around this immortal core and then to concentrate all immortal cores or centres around the core and centre of all things—this integral Yoga was an innovation and constituted a clear break with the traditional Sānkhya-Yoga which had made the sharpest distinction between Spirit and matter, the Imperishable and the perishable, Eternity and time. For Hinduism as a social structure he had no use at all, and the Vedānta of Śankara and Theravāda Buddhism he regarded as a *hīnayāna*, 'a defective way' at the best; but, having once discovered Hinduism, the national religion of India, he had no intention of leaving it. Indeed he had no incentive to do so, for Hinduism has no central authority to lay down what you should believe nor is it committed to any particular form of religious expression. Moreover, just as Teilhard found the justification for his radical re-interpretation of

Christianity in certain of the writings of St. Paul and St. John, so did Aurobindo find the justification for his dynamic inter-pretation of the Vedānta in the Hindu Scriptures themselves, particularly in the Bhagavad-Gītā and (less justifiably) in the Vedic Saṁhitās. He thus reversed the current monistic trend in Hindu mysticism by appealing to the sacred texts them-selves. Though he re-interpreted the Vedas along his own lines, he did in fact bring out their essential concern with *this* world which was a necessary corrective to the dominant in-wardness of the later Upanishads. The *Katha* Upanishad(4.1) had diverted man's eyes from the contemplation of the out-side world to his own hidden depths:

> The self-existent [Lord] bored holes facing the outside world:
> Therefore a man looks outward, not into himself.
> A certain sage, in search of immortality,
> Turned his eyes inward and saw the self within.

But the full teaching of the Upanishads is that 'without' and 'within' are one, the infinite and the infinitesimal meet and blend in the human heart, and both are pervaded and ruled by a 'Lord'. For had not the *Iśā* Upanishad (1) also said:

> This whole universe must be pervaded by a Lord,—
> Whatever moves in this moving [world].
> Abandon it, and then enjoy:
> Covet not the goods of anyone at all.

The essence of Aurobindo's thought is perhaps to be found in his *Thoughts and Aphorisms* compiled, apparently, in his old age. These derive almost entirely from the Hindu tradition, particularly the Bhagavad-Gītā and the *Bhāgavata* Purāna. Gone are the European influences, as are Aurobindo's own typical concepts of Supermind, Overmind and so on which appear to be central to his *magnum opus, The Life Divine,* but which in fact only duplicate the more traditional terminology, thereby creating unnecessary confusion. The same might be said about Teilhard with his Omega-point, noosphere, super-

humanity, super-Christ and so on—none of which is calculated to endear him to modern secular and scientific man
(for whom the terminology was presumably designed), let
alone to more traditional Christians.

Despite all this Teilhard, quite as much as Aurobindo, can
point to scriptural authority in support of his views. Taking
his stand on the assumption that the law of increasing entropy which must finally mean the death of the universe *must*
be counterbalanced by a complementary law of continually
increasing complexity-consciousness (the highest example of
which is up till now the human brain), he goes on to say (as
does Aurobindo) that the next stage of the evolution of this
planet will be the convergence of humanity upon itself, the
development, then, of a *collective* mind the nature of which
can be dimly inferred from the experience of cosmic consciousness. All this is to be found in St. Paul, 'not I' he admits,
'in the Sermon on the Mount or even in the gesture of the
Cross'[17],—that is to say, in an aspect of Christianity with
which Hindus on the whole are unfamiliar and which Aurobindo himself, despite his English education, either did not
know or preferred to ignore. This is St. Paul's vision of the
mystical body of Christ in the Church and of the cosmic
Christ he reveals in Philippians, Colossians, and Ephesians.
Through Christ and his Church the human race is destined
to grow together until 'everything is subjected to him, [and]
then the Son himself will be subject in his turn to the One
who subjected all things to him, so that God may be all
in all'[18]. This consummation of the whole human race
through the God-Man into God was God's purpose from the
beginning:

He has let us know the mystery of his purpose,
the hidden plan he so kindly made in Christ from the beginning
to act upon when the times had run their course to the end:
that he would bring everything together under Christ, as head,
everything in the heavens and everything on earth.[19]

---

[17] *Oeuvres* 6, p. 193.   [18] 1 Corinthians, 15, 28.   [19] Ephesians, 1. 9–10.

Now the Church is his body,
he is its head.[20]

These and passages like these are Teilhard's Bible, and he
certainly emphasizes them at the expense of all others. But
he was right to do so, for this aspect of Christianity had been
neglected and only through this approach, Teilhard thought,
could Christianity be made meaningful to modern man. He
saw Christ and Christianity in and through evolution—from
individuality through collectivity to a unity in diversity
centred on the cosmic Christ. This was precisely the vision of
Aurobindo in his *The Life Divine*. Substitute the Hindu
Trinity *sac-cid-ānanda* (Being—Logos—Joy) for Christ, and
the parallelism is exact. The difference is that, whereas Teilhard saw the instrument of human unity ready to hand in the
Church, Aurobindo could find no such principle of unity
within Hinduism since, socially, Hinduism has hitherto been
based on caste and even today the Śankarācārya of Puri can
defend not only the system of caste but also what Gandhi
called 'the ineffaceable blot' of untouchability. Even if we
are able to see merit in the caste system, its function is to
divide, not to unite, and what divides is, in the eyes of both
Teilhard and Aurobindo, evil. Acting on his own principle
that even a single soul fully integrated in the divine life must,
sooner or later, make its attraction felt throughout the entire
world, Aurobindo collected a few disciples around himself in
his Pondicherry ashram in the hope that, with the assistance
of a French lady whom he was bold enough to hail as the
Divine Mother and the eternal Śakti, he, the utterly perfected Siddha, would draw all things to himself. Since evolution works in units of millions rather than hundreds of years,
it is obviously very much too early to say whether he was
right.

To a convert to the Roman Catholic Church like myself it
seems odd that Aurobindo, and odder still that Teilhard
should have seen in Christianity a religion of renunciation

[20] Colossians, 1. 18.

and other-worldliness only. Making all allowances for over-simplification it is astonishing that so learned and widely-read a man as Aurobindo could have written:

Mediaeval Christianity said to the race, 'Man, thou art in thy earthly life an evil thing and a worm before God; renounce then egoism, live for the future state and submit thyself to God and His priest.' The results were not over-good for humanity. Modern knowledge says to the race, 'Man, thou art an ephemeral animal and no more to Nature than the ant and the earthworm, a transitory speck only in the universe. Live then for the State and submit thyself antlike to the trained administrator and the scientific expert.' Will this gospel succeed any better than the other?

Vedanta says rather, 'Man, thou art of one nature and substance with God, one soul with thy fellow-men. Awake and progress then to thy utter divinity, live for God in thyself and in others.' This gospel which was given only to the few, must now be offered to all mankind for its deliverance.[21]

Teilhard, on the other hand, sees what Aurobindo calls Vedānta in Christianity and what he calls Christianity in the Vedānta:

Once the distinction is recognized and the relative cosmic value of the two 'isotopes' of the Spirit appreciated, we can straightway classify and hence assess in terms of absolute value the leading religious tendencies which are now struggling for the consciousness of the Earth.

On the Eastern (Hindu) *side:* there can be no doubt that from the very beginning it has been the ideal of diffusion and identification that has been the dominant trend—individual egos being regarded as so many anomalies to be done away with (or holes to be filled up) in universal Being; or, what amounts to the same thing, in the eyes of the sage the biological evolution of the world is seen as no more than an illusion or as an insignificant eddy. Though this theme may be refurbished in minor detail, this is both the unchangeable essence and . . . the irremediable weakness of all mysticisms akin to the Vedānta.

On the Marxist side: I would go so far as to say that it is the Spirit of 'centration' which is quite clearly seeking expression in

[21] *Thoughts and Aphorisms*, p. 33.

the Communist drive to differentiate man and organize the earth on a higher level. I say 'seeking expression', and I mean it. But it will never be able to express itself adequately until the theoreticians of the Party bring themselves once and for all to endow the superstructure of the world with the same definitive coherence as they reserve for the material infrastructure of things.

On the Christian side we would make two observations, one affirmative and one restrictive. Both are necessary to do justice to the situation.

First of all and above all it is clear enough that it is towards the Spirit of unification and synthesis that Christianity has always found its point of equilibrium—and that in accordance with its very structure. Here God must at last become all in all (*tout en tous*) in an atmosphere of pure charity (*'sola caritas'*). In this magnificent definition of the pantheism of differentiation the very substance of the message of Jesus finds its unambiguous expression.[22]

Vedānta—Marxism—Christianity. In this at least Teilhard and Aurobindo agree: these, they think, are the only possible alternatives before mankind,—the three 'religions' of modern man. I have spoken of the Marxist alternative elsewhere and with considerable sympathy. Before referring to it again, however, I must draw your attention to one striking omission which here in India you cannot have failed to notice. I mean, of course, Islam.

Can we really write off Islam quite so easily even from the 'integral' and 'convergent' point of view of Teilhard and Aurobindo? It is true that Islam is having more trouble than any other religion in adapting itself to the modern world; but it is also true that in Muhammad Iqbal Islam has found its own Aurobindo. Progressives and conservatives are to be found in all religions and ideologies, and just as you have to set the Gandhis, Tagores, Aurobindos, and Radhakrishnans beside the unmoving ranks of the rigidly orthodox, and just as the tug-of-war between the conservatives and progressives has ever since the truly miraculous pontificate of good Pope John testified to the renewed vitality of the Roman Catholic

[22] Teilhard, *Oeuvres* 7, pp. 233–4.

Church, so too in Islam, throughout the last century and a half we have witnessed a continuous struggle between the reformers—the Afghanis, Abduhs, Sayyid Ahmad Khans, Amir Alis, and Iqbals—against the dead weight of traditional orthodoxy. Yet, whether Islam succeeds in modernizing itself or not, from the point of view of Teilhard and Aurobindo it shares with Catholicism one immense advantage: it has a principle and a locus of union. It has the Koran, the Word of God made Book, the Muslim equivalent of the Word made flesh, and it has Mecca, the physical centre and symbol of Muslim unity to which all Muslims turn in prayer and to which they make the statutory pilgrimage symbolizing their unity at least once in their lifetime if they possibly can. This is their point of union in space just as Jerusalem is for Jews and Christians alike. What it lacks is a point of union in time yet to be—the cosmic Christ of Teilhard's vision 'through whom and for whom God wanted . . . all things to be reconciled'. Islam may lack this, but then most Christians before Teilhard had long forgotten that they ever had it.

Besides these four, however,—Vedānta, Marxism, Christianity and Islam—there are usually reckoned to be five other 'great' religions of the world—Judaism, Zoroastrianism, Confucianism, Taoism, and Buddhism. Apart from a faithful remainder in India and Iran Zoroastrianism has long since perished by the sword of Islam; and the same fate has overtaken Confucianism, Taoism, and Buddhism in China at the hands of the revolutionary Marxism of Chairman Mao. Judaism, like Hinduism, remains the religion of a nation. Of its very nature it cannot become a world religion. There remains, then, only Buddhism—surely a great religion if ever there was one. Why, then, do neither Teilhard nor Aurobindo mention it? The reason is that for Teilhard it represents the same kind of spirituality as Śankara's Vedānta; it is not primarily interested in this world, while for Aurobindo its mysticism is altogether too negative—and dualist—for, in its Theravāda form, it draws far too sharp a distinction between Saṁsāra and Nirvāna, between time and eternity, this world which it dismisses as un-ease and that timeless condition in which there is no consciousness of this suffering world at all. But then, of course, there is Zen, and Zen is still the darling of the new America in search of its soul. Zen, however, would fall under the heading of Vedānta both for Aurobindo and for Teilhard. So far as its message can be expressed at all it is that 'all is One and One is all'; and that, after all, is the principal theme of the Upanishads. Zen, in fact, is cosmic consciousness, and cosmic consciousness is Zen. Zen, then, must form one element at least in the integral and convergent vision of Teilhard and Aurobindo. Indeed, had Teilhard read more widely, he would have realized this and might have hesitated to write with so superb a self-confidence these not very ecumenical words:

> The time has certainly arrived when at last, at the opposite pole of a dated orientalism, a new mysticism can and must emerge which will be both fully human and fully Christian: the highway of the West—the highway of the world of to-morrow.[23]

This is not untypical of Teilhard's rather condescending attitude towards Eastern mysticism, the less excusable perhaps in that he seems to have had no first-hand knowledge of it. This is the greater pity since he might have found there insights akin to his own and used them to strengthen his position against the legalist postures of Rome. This he for a moment realized when he met a missionary in China who assured him that 'there existed . . . the old Buddhist preoccupation to sound the rhythm of the world, to establish a perspective of its countless evolutions, to await the supreme Buddha who is to redeem all things. Such assurances,' he says, 'confirmed me in my old hope that we could perhaps learn from the mystics of the Far East how to make our religion more 'Buddhist' instead of being over-absorbed by ethics . . . and at last discover a Christ who is not only *a model of good conduct* and of '*humanity*', but the *superhuman* Being who, for ever in formation in the heart of the world, possesses a

[23] *Oeuvres* 7, p. 236.

being capable of bending all, and assimilating all, by vital domination.'[24]

This, so far as I know, is the only time that Teilhard refers sympathetically to Chinese Buddhism; and it seems very strange indeed that he should not have followed up this clue upon which he had stumbled. By and large his references to the non-Christian religions are uniformly unsympathetic, for he thinks of them as already having served their purpose. While admitting that Vedānta, by which he means all Hindu and Buddhist mysticism, is, together with Marxism, the only valid alternative to a revitalized and fully evolutionary Christianity, he sees in it only a reversion to a more primitive state of mind that may have existed before self-consciousness was born. It is not a broadening of consciousness directed towards a universal Centre which is for him the cosmic Christ but a merging and dissipation of the infant ego into the unconscious matter from which it had so laboriously evolved. It is essentially retrograde and the enemy of all progress.

When a man has emerged into consciousness of the cosmos and has deliberately flung himself into it, his first impulse is *to allow himself to be rocked* like a child by the great Mother in whose arms he has just awoken. For some this attitude of surrender is a mere aesthetic emotion, for others it is a rule of practical life, a system of thought, or even a religion; but in it lies the common root of all pagan pantheisms.

The essential revelation of paganism [by which Teilhard means Hinduism and Buddhism as well as nature mysticism in general] is that everything in the universe is uniformly true and valuable: so much so that the fusion of the individual must be effected with all things, *without distinction* and *without qualification*.[25]

This is in essence the mysticism of the earlier Upanishads. 'Whoso thus knows that he is Brahman becomes this whole [universe]: even the gods have not the power to cause him to un-Be, for he becomes their own self.'[26] This is to merge

---

[24] *Letters to Léontine Zanta* (E.T.), pp. 57–8.
[25] *Écrits du temps de la guerre*, p. 19: E.T., p. 28.
[26] *Brihadāranyaka* Upanishad, I. 4. 10.

back into the diffused state of primal matter, a state in which neither self-consciousness nor conscience has yet appeared: hence there is no sense of good and evil. To the man who has had this experience 'these two thoughts do not occur, "So I have done evil," or "So I have done good." He shrugs them off. What he has done and what he has left undone does not torment him.'[27] This is the eternal temptation or the eternal glory (as some might say) of Hinduism: for the man who is merged in cosmic consciousness, in Brahman, good and evil no longer have any meaning. This is quite brutally asserted in the *Kaushītakī* Upanishad (3. 1):

Indra did not swerve from the truth, for Indra *is* truth. So he said:

Know me, then, as I am. This indeed is what I consider most beneficial for mankind—that they should know me. I killed the three-headed son of Tvashtri, I threw the Arunmukha ascetics to the hyenas. Transgressing many a compact, I impaled the people of Prahlāda to the sky, the Paulomas to the atmosphere and the Kālakānjas to the earth, and I did not lose a single hair in the process.

The man who knows me as I am loses nothing that is his whatever he does, even though he should slay his mother or his father, even though he steal or procure an abortion. Whatever evil he does, he does not blanch.

But what is Brahman? Is it pure spirit, or is it merely undifferentiated matter? This we shall have to consider later. Whatever it may be, this transcending of good and evil in a state of undifferentiated oneness is typical of Hinduism but not, significantly, of Buddhism. Even the Gītā (18. 17) re-affirms the doctrine in no uncertain terms: 'A man who has reached a state in which there is no sense of "I", whose soul is undefiled—were he to slaughter all these worlds—slays nothing. He is not bound.' As Teilhard says, 'the fusion of the individual must be with all, *without distinction* and *without qualification*,' with what we generally regard as evil as well as

[27] Ibid., 4. 4. 22.

with what is obviously good. 'Everything that is active, that moves or breathes, every physical, astral, or animate energy, every fragment of force, every spark of life, is equally sacred; for in the humblest atom and the most brilliant star, in the lowest insect and the finest intelligence, there the *same Absolute* smiles and shudders.'[28] Yes, matter in its most simple and unevolved state is a strange enchantress, 'smiling at man with poetical, sensuous brightness,' as Marx[29] once said. This, Teilhard goes on to say, 'is the Eastern vision of the blue lotus, instinct with passion because every tangible beauty becomes godlike thereby, but heavy with matter whose dark recesses, stirred up by it, strive to rise up, to invade and absorb all spirituality.'

This is the secret of 'pagan' pantheism, a vision of the inter-connectedness of all things in matter which does away with all that is conscious and personal, sacrificing it all to 'the rudimentary and diffused modes of being' characteristic of emergent life. 'At first it would appear,' Teilhard goes on to say, 'that in the eyes of the Hindu *everything comes to life*; but, in reality, *everything is materialized*. The luminous destiny of all things, the paradise of which souls dream, *are confused with the dark source* from which they spring, with the fundamental reservoir of homogeneous ether and latent life into which everything must return and be lost, there to find its destined beatitude, for it is from there it came forth. *Life is understood and experienced as a function of matter.*'

This beatitude in primal matter Teilhard had himself experienced, and it is because he had experienced it that the distinction he consistently draws between 'the pantheism of identification at the opposite pole of love, "God is all," and the pantheism of unification beyond love, "God, whole in all things,"[30]' seems to have a compelling validity. Teilhard knew that his temperament was thoroughly pantheistic and he was not ashamed of it nor did he reject the experience out

---

[28] *Écrits du temps de la guerre*, ibid.
[29] *The Holy Family*, Moscow, 1956, p. 172.
[30] *Oeuvres* 7, pp. 231–2.

of hand: on the contrary, he considered that if his vision of a universe converging onto a personal Centre which is God were ever to be realized, then this could only begin with a generalization of cosmic consciousness in which all would begin to be aware of their connectedness with all things in the universe and in which 'each ego would find that it coincided . . . with the fullness of Being'[31]. The danger, as Aurobindo too realized, was that primal matter, primal energy, might be mistaken for absolute *Spirit*. In itself it is neither good nor evil, for matter is not concerned with morals any more than is science which seeks to understand and dominate it. For Teilhard, indeed, there is a sanctity in matter which claims and perhaps should not be denied adoration. 'To me, in my turn,' he says, 'as to all the sons of men it repeated the word which every generation hears; it was begging me to surrender myself unreservedly to it, and to worship it.'[32]

He succumbed to the temptation, and how he succumbed and surmounted it and saw it could be pressed into the service of the new evolutionary mysticism which he calls the 'mysticism of the West' he tells us with astonishing power in his little parable entitled *The Spiritual Power of Matter*,[33] ending as it does with a hymn to Matter itself, 'the stable, the great, the rich, the Mother, the Divine'[34].

The experience was overwhelming, but Teilhard refused to abandon himself entirely to its cosmic and all-embracing fascination. 'In the exhilaration of these first delights,' he writes,

I wanted to see whether, as the vast hopes aroused in my heart by 'the cosmic awakening' suggested, I could simply by surrendering to it reach the very heart of things, whether, by losing myself in its embrace, I could rediscover the soul of the world. Ardently and with no holding back I made the experiment, unable to imagine that the true could fail to coincide with this enchant-

[31] Ibid., p. 227.
[32] *Écrits du temps de la guerre*, p. 20: E.T., p. 29.
[33] *Écrits du temps de la guerre*, pp. 433–446: E.T. in *Hymn of the Universe*, pp. 59–71.
[34] *Écrits du temps de la guerre*, p. 20: E.T. *Writings in Time of War*, p. 29.

ment of the senses and this deadening of pain. And so it was that the more I allowed myself to flow ever closer towards the centre of primordial consciousness, becoming ever more expanded and dilated, the more I came to realize that the light of life was being darkened within me.

For one thing I felt less sociable. . . .

'For the pantheist to meet other men is painful,' because persons, being each the centre of their own private yet seemingly universal cosmos, are mutually exclusive; and 'it is the pantheist's dream to be, sufficiently unto himself (*adéquatement*), at one with all that surrounds him. So he isolates himself and becomes intoxicated with his isolation. When I recognized this symptom I realized that I was becoming less of a person, . . . and I was glad to see my responsibilities reduced. . . . I understood the meaning of the words [that matter] had spoken to me and which made the little-known depths of my being quiver in anticipation of a great and sanctifying calm; and I knew what it meant when it whispered, "Take the easier road." ' '

And so, Teilhard says, 'I [saw that I] had made a miserable mistake just now; I went completely astray when I yielded to the temptation of matter and relaxed the inner tension of my being and tried to extend myself throughout the universe, —boundlessly and without discernment. To grow in the truth we must travel with our backs turned to matter and not try to make contact with it once more so as to merge into it.'[35]

This merging into the material All Teilhard gratuitously identifies with the Buddhist Nirvāna which he seems to think is synonymous with 'effortless enjoyment', oblivious of the fact that one of the parts of the Noble Eightfold Path is 'right *effort*' and that Nirvāna, so far from being a merging into the infinite stream of matter, is, on the contrary, a total dissociation from all that is impermanent, that is, from matter itself. Moreover, Teilhard himself admits that only a greater diffusion of the 'cosmic sense' can point the way to the cosmic

[35] Ibid., pp. 21–23: E.T., pp. 30–32.

Christ whom he sees at the end of our heavenward journey. Hence he says:

> Son of man, bathe yourself in Matter. Dive into it where it is at its most violent and deep. Struggle in its current and drink of its waves. It is she who cradled you when you were yet unconscious; and it is she who will carry you right up to God.[36]

Teilhard is, then, quite wrong when he writes off Eastern mysticism as being 'dated'. Cosmic consciousness is something that is never dated since it recurs in individuals ever again. What he criticizes is only one tendency in Eastern mysticism, the tendency to renounce the world rather than to merge into it so as the better to dominate it.

He is right when he says that 'the incomparable greatness of the religions of the East lies in their having been second to none in vibrating with the passion for unity. This note, which is essential to every form of mysticism, has ever penetrated them so deeply that we find ourselves under a spell simply by uttering the names of their gods.'[37] But he is wrong when he adds that 'the Hindu sages thought that if man is to attain this unity he must renounce the earth, its passions and cares, and the efforts it demands'. For did not the *Iśā* Upanishad say: 'Renounce, and then *enjoy*.' And this is the message, much elaborated, it is true, not only of Aurobindo but also of Teilhard himself.

What Teilhard is attacking is Śankara's illusionism and the world-denying austerity of Theravāda Buddhism; but this is less than half of Indian religion, and this too was the object of Aurobindo's scarcely less stringent criticism. Both men, in fact, bring out an aspect of their own religion which had been neglected and both re-appraise their religions in the light of evolution; and both see only what is negative in the religion of the other. For what Aurobindo saw in Christianity was Evangelical Protestantism from which the mystical element was totally absent, while what Teilhard condemned in Indian

---

[36] *Écrits de temps de la guerre*, p. 442: E.T. in *Hymn of the Universe*, p. 65.
[37] *Oeuvres* 9, p. 138: E.T. *Science and Christ*, p. 105.

mysticism was 'a doctrine of passivity, of relaxation of tension, of withdrawal from things, . . . a doctrine in fact which is totally ineffective and dead'[38]. Aurobindo, on his side, while he could grant to Catholicism 'a tendency towards some conservation of the original plastic character of religion [and a] many-sidedness and appeal to the whole nature of the human being'[39], could only see in what Tillich has called 'the Protestant era' a *course à l'abîme* starting with the rejection of the very idea of Catholic wholeness and ending in spiritual suicide. For Protestantism was 'insistent on a pure reliance on belief, worship and conduct simplified so as to make a quick and ready appeal to the common reason, heart and ethical will. . . . [Of this] a certain dryness and a narrowness and paucity of the spiritual life have been a frequent consequence. Moreover, the intellect having denied so much, cast out so much, has found ample room and opportunity to deny more until it denies all, to negate spiritual experience and cast out spirituality and religion, leaving only intellect itself as the sole surviving power. But intellect void of the spirit can only pile up external knowledge and machinery and efficiency and ends in a drying up of the secret springs of vitality and a decadence without any inner power to save the life or create a new life or any other way out than death and disintegration.'[40]

Teilhard was wrong when he condemned Eastern mysticism as being 'totally ineffective and dead', but he was right when he said in a moment of truth that 'we could perhaps learn from the mystics of the Far East how to make our religion more "Buddhist" [that is, more inward] instead of being over-absorbed by ethics (that is to say too Confucianist)'[41], in other words more Protestant. Aurobindo too was right to condemn the rigidities of organized religion but wrong to imagine that his vision of the cosmos transformed

---

[38] *Oeuvres* 9, p. 138–9: E.T., p. 106.
[39] Aurobindo, *The Life Divine*, Pondicherry, 1955, p. 1037.
[40] Ibid., pp. 1037–8.
[41] Teilhard, *Letters to Léontine Zanta*, E.T., p. 58.

and re-integrated into the Divine could be realized except in the framework of a religious organization capable of transforming itself into a living organism in which the individual parts would depend for their life on the whole, each contributing its own special excellence to the well-being of the total body which one day would embrace all mankind. And yet, when he thought of it at all, he realized that the Catholic principle within Christianity was the nearest approximation in the history of religions to his own vision of a humanity redeemed and divinized. In the West, he thought, the Reformation, with its rejection of the physical unity of the Church, had strangled man's natural drive towards unity which is the mainspring of Eastern religion, thus alienating him both from the immanent God within him and from his own immortal soul. Had this not happened, 'it would have been possible for the evolutionary principle to have preserved its pristine wholeness of movement while pressing on, by an expansion and not a disruption of the wiser ancient harmony, to a greater synthesis of the principle of concentration and the principle of diffusion.'[42]

Teilhard and Aurobindo, then, are united in their mistrust of formalist and legalistic religion, in their insistence on the primacy of the mystical life, and in their belief that evolution is nothing less than the ascent from the kingdom of matter to the kingdom of spirit through man who is the bridge between the two. For the one the only possible vehicle for this ascent is the Catholic Church, for the other it is the Vedānta as re-interpreted by himself. This much at least is clear: so far as what Teilhard called *le dedans des choses*, 'the inward aspect of things,' is concerned, the two men are at one. What of the outward aspect, the social side of the purely human phase of evolution? This 'outward' aspect of the evolutionary process which must be called in to supplement what Teilhard calls Vedānta and Aurobindo calls Christianity is the drive towards socialized unity, towards Marxian Communism, if you like, in which 'the free

[42] Aurobindo, *The Life Divine*, p. 1038.

development of each will be the condition for the free development of all'. The unifying power of Communism had always exercised a powerful fascination on Teilhard, and in the conflict between the Communists and the Kuo Min Tang in China his sympathies were with the former, for in them he saw 'the "birth" of a new human group that nothing can prevent'[43]. Indeed, whether we like it or not, a new world is coming to birth before our eyes:

> *har sūy bāng ō mashghalé, har kūy shamᶜ ō mashᶜalé,*
> *k'emshab jahān ē ḥāmelé zāyad jahān ē jāvedān!*

> Wherever you look there is the din of tumult,
> Wherever you go there are candles and torches,
> For to-night this world is heavy and in travail,
> Striving to give birth to an eternal world.

So said the Persian poet and mystic Jalālu 'd-dīn Rūmī, and what he prophesied is taking shape before our very eyes. Something tremendous is happening, something as disruptive and tormenting as the birth of a child. How and when will the child be born? And what kind of child will it be? For Teilhard it was the birth of the new collective Man. 'Look:' he cried out, 'we just can't breathe in our different compartments, our closed categories. Without destroying our more limited organisms, we must fuse them together, synthetize them: man, nothing but man, nothing less than man as the context of our ambitions and organizations.'[44] Nothing less than man, the new Man for whom all the religions have been waiting:

> *k'emshab jahān ē ḥāmelé zāyad jahān ē jāvedān.*

> For to-night this world is heavy and in travail,
> Striving to give birth to an eternal world.

Perhaps some of us will live to see this new collective man. Or perhaps he will be still-born.

[43] Teilhard, op. cit., p. 78.   [44] Ibid., p. 79.

II

A WORLD IN TRAVAIL

Emshab jahān ē ḥāmelé zāyad jahān ē jāvedān.

Tonight this world is heavy and in travail,
Striving to give birth to an eternal world.

THAT we are living in a time of troubles is so obvious as
to be barely worth mentioning. Can it be true that
these troubles, these wars and stresses and frustrations,
are in reality the birth-pangs of a new, a better, and a
different world? To the very last Teilhard, against all the
evidence of two world wars and an armed armistice only
maintained by a balance of terror, believed that the spirit of
man was on the verge of a break-through to a new form of
socialized and 'totalized' existence. Aurobindo could not entirely share this optimism to the end, for his ashram in Pondicherry had not yet given birth to new centres in which what
he called Supermind could manifest itself. This was perhaps a
disappointment to him since, unlike Teilhard, he saw himself as the divine centre from which the transformation of man
into 'super-manhood' was to radiate. During the thirty years
in which he had been engaged in 'bringing down the Supramental' nothing much had happened outwardly: the ashram
was indeed and still is a going and expanding concern, but
its impact on the world has so far been slight and is not yet
comparable to that of the widely diffused Ramakrishna
Mission. But then Aurobindo, like Teilhard, could always fall
back on the theory of evolution itself and the prodigious
periods of time that it presupposes. Thus to an impatient
disciple he says:

What would have satisfied your rational mind—3 years? 3
months? 3 weeks? Considering that by ordinary evolution it

could not have been done even at Nature's express speed in less than 3000 years, and would ordinarily have taken anything from 30,000 to 3,000,000, the transit of 30 years is perhaps not too slow.[1]

The earth had, indeed, not proved responsive to the divine transformation that was to have become manifest through him. Hence he had no alternative but to give up his body quite voluntarily—or so his disciples believe—'in an act of supreme unselfishness ... to hasten the hour of collective realization'[2]. In 1915 he had said: 'Heaven we have possessed, but not the earth; but the fullness of the Yoga is to make ... Heaven and earth equal and one,'[3] But it needs much more than one lifetime to do this.

Aurobindo had once been a revolutionary and was therefore intensely interested in the political developments of his time. Just as he thought that the religions in modern times could be classed as Vedāntin (that is, his own integral Yoga which was to result in the transformation and spiritualization of humanity through the descent of Supermind), Christian (which he identified with a world-denying asceticism), and Communist (the cult, he thought, of the collective at the expense of the individual); so too in the purely political field he saw three forces at work,—the three principles of the French Revolution,—liberty, equality, and fraternity. The French revolutionaries, he thought, were ahead of their time in trying to combine these three principles since they were mutually incompatible. Liberty, was not compatible with equality while fraternity implied a radical reversal of man's ingrained egoistic tendency which no amount of liberty or equality could bring about. However, the Revolution could be regarded as the dawn of the age of reason which is a necessary prelude to the age of collectivized humanity which will be inaugurated by the descent of Supermind into the human mass.

If [he said] we may judge from the modern movement, the

---

[1] *A Practical Guide to Integral Yoga*, Pondicherry, 1955, p. 389.
[2] Ibid., p. 442.   [3] Above p. 8.

progress of the reason as a social renovator and creator, if not interrupted in its course, would be destined to pass through three successive stages which are the very logic of its growth, the first individualistic and increasingly democratic with liberty for its principle, the second socialistic, in the end perhaps a governmental communism with equality and the State for its principle, the third—if that ever gets beyond the stage of theory—anarchistic in the higher sense of that much-abused word, either a loose voluntary co-operation or a free communalism with brotherhood or comradeship and not government for its principle. It is in the transition to its third and consummating stage, if or whenever that comes, that the power and sufficiency of the reason will be tested; it will then be seen whether the reason can really be the master of our nature, solve the problems of our inter-related and conflicting egoisms and bring about within itself a perfect principle of society or must give way to a higher guide. For till this third stage has its trial, it is Force that in the last resort really governs. Reason only gives to Force the plan of its action and a system to administer.[4]

There is much wisdom in this analysis of our present predicament. As Aurobindo says elsewhere speaking in purely Hindu terms, the French and American revolutions marked the end of the condominium of the Brahmins and Kshatriyas and ushered in the reign of the Vaiśyas: they put an end, that is to say, to the alliance between Church and State and replaced it by the rule of the capitalistic bourgeoisie. The emergence of the bourgeoisie as the principal property-owning class makes the conflict between capital and labour, between the 'haves' and the 'have-nots', inevitable. The turn of the Śūdras has come[5]. This 'transvaluation' of all values had long ago been prophesied in the *Mahābhārata*[6], but so far from being welcomed it was regarded as being the ultimate evil and the prelude to the end of the world. Thus in his social thinking Aurobindo, like all progressive Hindu thinkers, makes a clean break with traditional values. Social-

---

[4] *The Human Cycle*, ch. 19 (*The Human Cycle* etc., Pondicherry, 1962, p. 259).
[5] *The Ideal of Human Unity*, ch. 25 in *The Human Cycle* etc., p. 647.
[6] 3. 188.

ism or Communism is a necessary, even if painful, stage on man's journey from unorganized matter towards the Divine. It is certainly not the harbinger of the final calamity. In the last days, the *Mahābhārata* again says, all men will become *mlecchas*,—the whole world will be secularized, and this is precisely what is happening before our very eyes. For anyone with any sense of tradition this is bound to be a painful process; but pain and failure are inseparable from progress just as there is no childbirth without the pangs of parturition. Yes, 'the earth is in travail now of one, common, large and flexible civilization for the whole human race into which each modern and ancient culture shall bring its contribution and each clearly defined human aggregate shall introduce its necessary element of variation.'[7]

This had been the ideal of Marx and Engels too. The dictatorship of the proletariat which, contrary to all their ideas, turned out to be the dictatorship not even of the Communist Party but of a tiny oligarchy within it, was to have given way to a free society in which the state would have withered away. 'The possibility of securing for every member of society,' Engels had written, 'by means of socialized production, an existence not only sufficient materially, and becoming day by day more full, but an existence guaranteeing to all the free development and exercise of their physical and mental faculties—this possibility is now for the first time here, but *it is here*.'[8] This he had forecast on the basis of Marx's dialectical analysis of the bourgeois-proletarian antithesis and the eventual and inevitable emergence of a synthesis in which 'the free development of each would be the condition for the free development of all'. Aurobindo was less naive than this, for he realized that man, so long as he is a slave to his own egoism, can scarcely be expected to relinquish power once he has it in his grasp. The classless society prophesied by Marx and Engels could, on purely rational grounds alone, scarcely come into being so long as men remained what

[7] *The Ideal of Human Unity*, ch. 6 in *The Human Cycle* etc., p. 419.
[8] Engels, *Socialism Utopian and Scientific*, end.

hitherto, with some shining exceptions, they have always been,—egoists. Hence 'it is not likely that [any] living [Socialist] State machine once in power . . . would let go its prey or allow itself to be abolished without a struggle.'[9] How then is the human race to emerge from 'this perpetual cycle of failure'[10]? In *The Life Divine* Aurobindo sees the solution in a descent of 'Supermind' which will reveal to the world that it has a common soul, present and the same in all but differentiated in each. But how is this ideal of true anarchy and true fraternity to be achieved? There is really only one answer, and that has hitherto always eluded the human race. Reason on its own is useless, for the first function of discursive thought is to separate, not to unite, to analyse not to synthetize. What unites is not reason but love. 'A deeper brotherhood, a yet unfound law of love is the only sure foundation possible for a perfect social evolution, no other can replace it.'[11] Very true, but as Aurobindo himself points out elsewhere, brotherhood itself is a very ambivalent affair; for in the Hebrew legend it starts with Cain and Abel, the murder of the just.

Modern experience has not been encouraging, and it can at least be argued that the history of the Western world has become more troubled, more cruel, and certainly more fanatical since the Prince of Peace announced that he had come to bring not peace but the sword. Obviously if the Christian claim is true and God became man at a given moment of time, then something momentous must have happened. But where is the evidence for this? Can we truthfully say that the advent of the Christ and the establishment of Christianity has in any way changed or embellished the face of the earth? On the contrary, since the appearance of Christianity not only has brother continued to kill brother, but brotherhood has slaughtered and persecuted brotherhood in the name of Christ himself. In this particular form of beastliness Christianity has won for itself a unique distinction.

[9] Aurobindo, *The Human Cycle* etc., p. 272, n. 1.
[10] Ibid., p. 299.   [11] Ibid., ch. 20, p. 296.

In a brilliant phrase Aurobindo once said: 'Man is an abnormal who has not found his own normality.'[12] And he
knows it; for whereas all other creatures seem to follow
effortlessly their own law, from the galaxies to the most insignificant insects and plants on this earth of ours, man alone
seems to be perpetually alienated from himself and astray.
The religions of the world have all offered solutions for the
dilemma of mankind, they have all sought to devise a
specifically human 'law', a human *dharma* or human *Tao*,
and none has in the long run succeeded. In China the Confucians tried to integrate man into the natural rhythm of
things by inserting him as the mid-point of a trinity the poles
of which were heaven and earth. In India the Brahmins
sought to establish a hierarchy of social classes in which each
should carry out his own predestined task; but however
suitable this social structure may have been for the society
in which it originated, it was later to give birth to the mons-
trous inequalities of the caste system which Mahatma Gandhi
was later so vigorously to denounce. In Palestine Jesus had
announced a *new* law of love:

> I give you a *new* commandment:
> love one another;
> just as I have loved you,
> you also must love one another.[13]

Notice that he said that he brought a *new* commandment.
Since Cain murdered Abel men have not loved one another.
In China the Confucians thought that Mo Tze was both mad
and immoral when he preached a doctrine of universal love;
for how could any sane person be expected to extend the circle
of his love beyond his own family? Love is a carefully graded
affair, starting from the family and extending itself in ever-
diminishing ripples to the confines of the whole Empire. Beyond that there are only the barbarians, and to love *them*
would scarcely befit a Confucian gentleman. It is this
particularization of love that has always and everywhere

---

[12] Ibid., ch. 22, p. 315.   [13] John, 13. 34.

bedevilled human relationships. The love of *God*, indeed, is not only the first commandment of the Old Testament; it is also Krishna's final and 'most mysterious' revelation in the Bhagavad-Gītā. But to love one's fellow-men is quite another matter, and few have found it easy. The Sanskrit word *bhakti* means both love and loyalty; but even loyalty has proved difficult to maintain except in the face of a common enemy; and now that thanks to rapid communications and the mass media, the world is visibly converging on itself, we do not actually tear each other limb from limb, not through any mutual affection we might feel for one another but through an equipoise of terror which holds us for a little while in check. Our national egos, as Aurobindo called the nation states, have been somewhat sobered by the last World War, but they are virulently active still. The British Empire of which, in so far as it unified a large part of the human race, Aurobindo approved, but which, in so far as this union was imposed by force, he found intolerable, has disintegrated. So too has the French. It may be that this achievement of liberty by the peoples once held in unnatural thraldom by the champions of liberty themselves has generated a minimum of fraternal feeling, but from the point of view of the unification of mankind, it looks like a retrograde step; for we now lack any centre of cohesion to which even the members of the Commonwealth can look.

The religions, Aurobindo thought, had served their purpose, and he may have been right; but they provided a frame of reference to whole sections of mankind. If the religions are dead or dying, then nothing has yet come to take their place —except perhaps science, as Teilhard would have us believe.

Man is a microcosm in which is or should be reflected the harmony of the spheres; and if individual men are capable of reflecting this cosmic harmony, should they not be able to reproduce it among their fellow-men? And was it not a sign of an inner despair that Aurobindo retreated into himself during the last twenty years of his life? 'Heaven we have possessed,' he had said, 'but not the earth;' but despite the theoretical dynamism of his philosophy which was to have transformed Hinduism, when he died he had still not succeeded in 'making Heaven and earth equal and one'. Perhaps he has left behind in his ashram not only the 'kingdom of God within us' but also, however small it may be, a 'city of God upon earth'[14].

And yet he realized that without an inner transformation of the individual there could be no outer transformation of the collectivity. The imposition of socialism by force could not be the solution; and this is why the Soviet experience has been so tragic and bloodthirsty a failure. This is simply to substitute a communal for an individual ego,—an inflated *ahaṁkāra* masquerading as the Self of the All, 'a forced compression and imposed unanimity of mind and life and a mechanical organization of the communal existence. A unanamity of this kind can only be maintained by a compression of all freedom of thought and life, and that must bring about either the efficient stability of a termite civilization or a drying up of the springs of life and a swift or slow decadence.'[15]

If Soviet Russia were a truly Communist and Marxist state in which individual and state combined to build an 'association in which the free development of each was the condition for the free development of all', then Aurobindo's ideal would have been at least partially fulfilled. But even so only partially; for 'the solution lies not in the reason but in the soul of man. ... It is a spiritual, an inner freedom that can alone create a perfect human order. ... A deeper brotherhood, a yet unfound law of love is the only sure foundation possible for a perfect social evolution, ... a love which is founded upon a deeper truth of our being, the brotherhood or, let us say, ... the spiritual comradeship which is the expression of an inner realization of oneness. For only so can egoism disappear and the true individualism of the unique godhead in each man found itself on the true communism of the equal

[14] *The Human Cycle* etc., p. 165.   [15] *The Life Divine*, p. 1256.

godhead in the race; for the Spirit, the inmost Self, the universal Godhead in every being is that whose very nature of diverse oneness it is to realize the perfection of its individual life and nature in the existence of all.'[16]

This was the hope of Aurobindo, but he was usually clear-sighted enough to see that there was always a chance that it might fail, and in any case things had to be seen in terms of evolutionary time, not in terms of human generations.

'This,' he goes on to say, 'is a solution to which it may be objected that it puts off the consummation of a better human society to a far-off date in the future evolution of the race. For it means that no machinery invented by the reason can perfect either the individual or the collective man; an inner change is needed in human nature, a change too difficult to be ever effected except by the few. This is not certain; but in any case, if this is not the solution, then there is no solution; if this is not the way, then there is no way for the human kind.'

Usually, however, Aurobindo is little given to pessimism; for he regards the evolutionary process as inevitably leading back to the supreme *Sac-cid-ānanda*, the triune God who is not only the static God of the philosophers but also a *living* God who operates in time. More concretely he sees evolution both in political terms and in terms of ever greater awareness—a progression from apparently inanimate matter to life, from life to consciousness and mind, from mind to what he calls Overmind, and from Overmind to Supermind which, if I understand him aright, is pure *cit*, pure consciousness, operating in the world as *śakti* or power. This ascent from matter to Spirit he sometimes sees as a return to the insights already 'given' in the Upanishads and Veda. 'We have then to *return* to the pursuit of an ancient secret which man, as a race, has seen only obscurely and followed after lamely, has indeed understood only with his surface mind and not in its heart of meaning—and yet in following it lies his social no less than his individual salvation—the ideal of the Kingdom

[16] *The Human Cycle* etc., ch. 20, pp. 295–6.

of God, the secret of the reign of the Spirit over mind and life and body.'[17]

But Aurobindo is not consistent in this. Sometimes he speaks of an 'original innocence' in which man is guided by 'intuition', the sense of oneness which lies at the heart of the Upanishads. This gives way to rational knowledge, first to metaphysical thinking and then to experimental science.[18] This progress is both a rise and a fall—a rise in the sense that the individual must discover that he has an existence of his own, but a fall in the sense that he comes to imagine that his own individual existence is independent of the sum of existence and that he is free to exert it for his own exclusive benefit and at the expense of others. This is the original ignorance and the original sin of mankind—the ignorance and the sin of the ego folded in upon itself. Anything that brings the individual out of his pure ego-centricity is therefore an advance even if it means only the creation of a wider 'ego'—the family, tribe, nation, or church. These, though adumbrations of a final collective mystical intuition, are still inward-looking and not the final goal which in any case can only be spiritual. Yet even so, on the purely exoteric level too, whatever works towards union is a step in the right direction —socialism, for instance, in the field of politics and science in the field of rational activity.

It must be remembered that there is Aurobindo the socialist and Aurobindo the mystic. The first is typified in *The Human Cycle* and *The Ideal of Human Unity*, while the second unfolds himself at enormous length in *The Life Divine*. Though he continually speaks of his 'integral Yoga' which is supposed to contain both, the two aspects of him, the exoteric concerned with the building of the city of God on earth and the esoteric struggling to realize the kingdom of God within you, tend to drift apart, the latter tending to assume greater importance in his later work. Unlike Teilhard his background was literary, not scientific, and his attitude towards science remains ambivalent. Very occasionally he sees science as the

[17] Ibid., ch. 22, p. 322.   [18] *The Life Divine*, p. 82.

great unifier of the human race as, for example, in the following passage which might well have been written by Teilhard:

There are many conditions and tendencies in human life at present which are favourable to the progress of the internationalist idea. The strongest of these favourable forces is the constant drawing closer of the knots of international life, the multiplication of points of contact and threads of communication and an increasing community in thought, in science and in knowledge. Science especially has been a great force in this direction; for science is a thing common to all men in its conclusions, open to all in its methods, available to all in its results: it is international in its very nature; there can be no such thing as a national science, but only the nations' contributions to the work and growth of science which are the indivisible inheritance of all humanity.[19]

Passages like this are, however, exceptional, for on the whole Aurobindo mistrusted science and particularly medical science for which he had an irrational and obscurantist aversion.[20] His tribute to it, such as it is, seems to be only lip-service paid to a fashionable idol. In this he differs widely from Teilhard for whom scientific research was akin to adoration[21] and who could say: 'Neither in its impetus nor in its achievements can science go to its limits without becoming tinged with mysticism and charged with faith.'[22]

Yet despite the differences between the two men they share a common view of the universe. First, Spirit takes precedence over matter. Secondly, since this is so, it follows that Spirit must always have been in matter in a rudimentary form. Third, evolution is a progressive unification, an ever-increasing spiritualization of matter. Fourth, the goal of evolution must be the integration of matter in a final harmony and its convergence on to a centre of attraction which is supramental and divine. Fifthly, the only conceivable agent

[19] *The Ideal of Human Unity* in *The Human Cycle* etc., ch. 32, pp. 736–7.
[20] See *Thoughts and Aphorisms*, pp. 62–6.
[21] Teilhard de Chardin, *The Phenomenon of Man*, E.T., p. 250.
[22] Ibid., p. 284.

of such a convergence is a 'yet unfound law of love'. Both men again were profoundly dissatisfied with their own religions as currently practised and interpreted and sought to re-construct them in an evolutionary mould. Both again regarded suffering and strife as being of the very stuff of evolutionary progress; and both of them at times seem singularly callous in their attitude to individual and unmerited suffering. Aurobindo is particularly harsh in his attitude to suffering and cruelty, and in this he is true to one side of the Hindu tradition—true too, it must be said, to the idea of divinity portrayed in much of the Old Testament. Few other thinkers would have dared to say that 'this world was built by Cruelty that she might love'[23], or that 'God justifies himself in the end even when He has masked Himself as a bully and a tyrant'[24].

Aurobindo had said: 'An inner change is needed in human nature, a change too difficult to be ever effected except by the few.' The liberator must himself be liberated if he is to effect the liberation of others. And Aurobindo would not have been a Hindu if 'liberation'—the emancipation of pure timeless spirit from the multiplicities of matter—had not played a leading part in his thought. Both he and Teilhard evolved a system founded on mystical experience and developed it along evolutionary lines. Both might be regarded as Gnostics, for both, in their different ways, interpret the 'Fall' in a cosmic sense: Spirit 'falls' into matter and its true nature is thereby 'veiled' from itself. On the nature of this 'Fall' Aurobindo is confused; but in *The Life Divine* his thought seems to be nearest to Neo-Platonism among the philosophies of the West. The supreme Absolute which in itself must be beyond change is the classic *Sac-cid-ānanda*—Being, Consciousness, and Joy, an almost exact counterpart of the Christian Trinity as we shall see—absolutely One in itself but nonetheless containing the seed of multiplicity. From this Trinity, or more specifically from Consciousness indwelt by Joy proceeds Supermind which he also calls

[23] *Thoughts and Aphorisms*, p. 14.   [24] Ibid., p. 82.

Consciousness-Force; in Christian terminology we might say the Logos in its creative action. From this proceeds Overmind which is the boundary between the 'pleroma' of pure Being and the world of becoming, the universe, that is, in which we live. Thus 'Overmind stands at the top of the lower hemisphere'[25]; below is what Aurobindo calls the world of the Ignorance which consists of mind, life, and finally matter. This descent of Spirit into matter he calls devolution, the necessary obverse of evolution. In 'inconscient' matter as he calls it Spirit had become totally submerged: it is not aware of itself, or, if you prefer it, it is playing hide-and-seek with itself, the divine 'game' so beloved of the Hindus. Matter, however, though the form of existence the most remote from the divine Absolute since it neither is (it only becomes), nor is it conscious, nor does it experience joy, is at the same time pregnant with life and later with consciousness and joy: it is therefore the source of individuality. Individuality differentiates, but it is not for this reason evil; for, as Teilhard says, 'union differentiates' in the sense that 'in every organized whole, the parts perfect themselves and fulfil themselves'[26]. Phenomenal man, then, is matter (body) plus life plus consciousness or mind. This is his evolutionary nature. But this is only part of the story, since evolution is the obverse of devolution, and man is liable to get stuck in the 'lower hemisphere' which has Overmind as its ceiling, if there is no outpouring of Supermind, of cosmic consciousness and joy— of the Holy Spirit, we might say—to help it on its way.

This 'lower hemisphere' is dominated by the rational and discursive mind, again not evil in itself, but necessarily restrictive, for minds in so far as they are associated with matter in the human brain, are necessarily attached to an ego, and it is the ego that divides and prevents us from seeing the whole universe as an interconnected and harmonious whole centred through the channel of Supermind on to the un- divided Trinity from which it proceeds. The ego, then, is the

[25] *A Practical Guide to Integral Yoga*, p. 385.
[26] *The Phenomenon of Man*, E.T., p. 262

villain of the piece, for original Ignorance or original sin consists in identifying oneself with the body and mind rather than with the immortal 'person' which is eternal and a 'part' of God as the Gītā puts it (15. 7). Because it has been preceded by devolution, a veiling of the divine Spirit in matter, evolution must have a goal; but the goal is not a simple return to the *status quo ante* but a diversification and as it were a completion of the divine Trinity itself by bringing back to it all that had apparently been lost. This cannot be done until each individual realizes that he is not an independent ego acting of his own free will, but an interdependent person deriving his personality from God, wholly indwelt by God, possessed of his eternal Being, his eternal Consciousness, and his eternal Joy, and through this 'sameness' of nature which all beings derive from God, at one with all created things, and so acting and knowing that he acts not on his own account but entirely in accordance with the will of God. But before this stage can be reached the ego must be destroyed; and this means the destruction of what we have all along considered to be our personality, we must depersonalize ourselves, give up self as the Buddhists are bidden to do and enter into the timeless bliss of Nirvāna, faring 'like the horn of a rhinoceros alone'[27], 'isolated' and 'unconditioned' as are the *purushas* of the Sānkhya-Yoga. This is the boundary between the upper and lower hemispheres of existence, and it is here that one finds *requiem aeternam*, 'eternal rest'. But, as Aurobindo points out again and again, this is not the end as Śankara had supposed, identifying the oneness of each 'part' of God with the totality of God himself: for this is to realize Being only, beyond becoming. God, however, is not just a static monad but a *living* and therefore dynamic reality: for does not the *Iśā* Upanishad (5) say:

> It moves. It does not move.
> It is far, yet it is near.
> It is within this whole universe,
> And yet it is without it.

[27] *Suttanipāta*, 35ff.

To attain to Nirvāna is to become Brahman, to pass beyond space and time into an unconditioned form of existence. From this vantage-point the Yogin sees his 'self in all beings standing, all beings in the self: the same in everything he sees.'[28] This is cosmic consciousness, the discovery that through the Eternal one is interconnected with all things. But one must then go on to the further realization that this interconnectedness, though deriving from the same impersonal One, nevertheless does not mean complete identity or absorption, but leads on to the discovery of a new relationship with a personal God on whom the impersonal Absolute itself depends.

Who, standing firm on unity communes in love with me as abiding in all beings, in whatever state he be, that integrated man abides in me.[29]

So says the Gītā; and as Aurobindo points out, this depersonalizing process, this loss of all sense of self in the still waters of eternity in which all passion is quenched, love quite as much as hate—this depersonalizing process is only the necessary prelude to the resurrection in God and for God in love.

You must love the Lord your God with all your heart, with all your soul, and with all your mind. This is the greatest and the first commandment. The second resembles it: You must love your neighbour as yourself.[30]

It was Jesus who first brought these two commandments together. They do not make easy reading for the mystic; for the mystic, if he does not stop within the eternal peace of Nirvāna or at the vision of the cosmic Self through which he can 'extend himself throughout the universe—boundlessly and without discernment'[31], must then, under the afflatus of what Aurobindo calls Supermind, be turned toward the triune God himself, and, being turned towards him, love him to the

---

[28] Bhagavad-Gītā, 6. 29.   [29] Ibid., 6. 31.
[30] Matthew, 22. 37–9.   [31] Above, p.22.

exclusion of all else. This seems to preclude love of one's neighbour, and this is indeed emphatically affirmed by the bulk of the mystics of all religions. True, *sāmya*, the 'sameness and indifference' which, according to the Gītā (5. 19) is the essence of the eternal Brahman, implies a general benevolence towards all creatures (5. 25), but this is very far from the positive love demanded by Christ in the New Testament. This is not surprising, for altruistic love in the best sense has for nearly two thousand years been no more than a pious fiction assiduously preached from the pulpit and as assiduously evaded in our daily life. Both Aurobindo and Teilhard, realizing, with Heraclitus, that evolutionary progress which in all its phases means ever-increasing union in ever-increasing complexity—a work of love, then, since it is love that unites—cannot be achieved without strife and suffering and the elimination of much waste-matter in the process: hence they rarely discuss the possibility of the love of man for his neighbour until society itself has become, to use Marx's expression once more, 'an association in which the *free* development of each is the condition for the *free* development of all'.

'Free': in Sanskrit this would be *mukta*: and, to adapt the Marxian phrase to the Hindu-Christian context in which we are now moving, 'freedom' of the spirit from all attachment to matter is the condition for the further development of spirits and for their collaboration in the further task of building up a 'spiritual house' compacted of 'living stones'[32].

Such spirits, however, who will have the knowledge and skill to act as midwives to the 'eternal world', the 'city of God on earth', are, according to Aurobindo, few and far between; for, despite some radiant exceptions of which the latest was surely the well-beloved Pope John XXIII, men have not learnt to love their neighbour as themselves. This is not surprising, for Christianity itself is as yet, in terms of evolutionary time, a babe in arms; for if it is true that 'with the Lord a day can mean a thousand years, and a thousand years

[32] Cf. 1 Peter, 2. 5.

is like a day'[33], then the Church is not yet quite two days old. So how can you expect it even to *understand* Christ's *new* commandment at so tender an age? She must love God, for she is as dependent on him as is an infant on its mother; but how can she or her members be expected to love their neighbour as themselves? And yet the dual command remains and is repeated even more starkly by St. John:

Anyone who says, 'I love God',
and hates his brother,
is a liar,
since the man who does not love the brother he can see
cannot love God, whom he has never seen.[34]

It would then seem that the great majority of us are liars; for, as Teilhard says, 'Man's capacity . . . is confined to giving his affection to one human being or to very few. Beyond that radius the heart does not carry, and there is only room for cold justice and cold reason. To love all and everyone is a contradictory and false gesture which only leads in the end to loving no-one.'[35] Teilhard, by all accounts, was an unusually attractive and charitable man, but even so to him love of one's neighbour did not come naturally. To love those who love you, he knew, was easy, but this was not a love for which anyone could claim credit, for 'even the tax-collectors do as much'[36]; but to love one's neighbour in general, that is to say, every Tom, Dick, and Harry who crosses your path, could he or anyone else truthfully say that he had succeeded? In a deeply disquieting passage in *Le milieu divin* he writes:

Once a man has fallen in love with the divine *milieu*, he cannot bear the darkness, tepidity, and emptiness he sees on every side in what ought to be filled with God and pulsating in him. At the very idea of the countless spirits bound to him in the unity of the same world but not yet kindled in the fire of the divine presence, he feels himself as it were stiff with cold.

O God, I confess to you that I have long been and still am im-

<hr>

[33] 2 Peter, 3. 8.   [34] 1 John, 4. 20.
[35] *The Phenomenon of Man*, E.T., p. 266.   [36] Matthew, 5. 46.

pervious to the love of my neighbour. The more ardently I have tasted of the superhuman joy of being broken and lost in the souls to which some mysterious affinity of human love had predestined me, the more I feel hostile and closed to the common run of those you bid me love—and that is something I seem to be born with. What is above me or below me in the universe,... matter, plants, animals, and then Powers, Dominations, Angels— these I can accept without difficulty and rejoice in feeling myself supported in the hierarchy they represent. But the 'other', my God, by which I mean not only 'the poor, the lame, the twisted, the plain stupid', but simply the other, the other *tout court*—the other who seems to live independently of me in a universe apparently closed to mine and who, as far as I am concerned, shatters the unity and the silence of the world—would I be sincere if I were not to tell you that my instinctive reaction is to fight him off, and that the very idea of entering into spiritual communion with him disgusts me.[37]

This is a terrible confession, but most of us must feel that it is true of us too.

> I give you a new *commandment*,
> love one another.

This is surely the most extraordinary commandment ever given; for love is not love at all if it is not spontaneous. How, then, can it be commanded? The answer, however, appears in the next sentence:

> Just as I have loved you,
> you also must love one another.

Christ loved the twelve not for their own sake, but because they had returned his love: they had consented to be loved by the God who is Love itself. Hence to love one another is to love in and through Christ. As Teilhard says: 'The very idea of entering into spiritual communion with' one 'who seems to live independently of me in a universe apparently closed to mine' 'is disgusting', because Christ, the connecting link, is not felt to be present.

This is the language of the mystic from whom it is required

[37] *Oeuvres* 4, pp. 183–5: E.T., *The Divine Milieu*, pp. 137–8.

that he should love God to the exclusion of all else. Through God he can come to love the universe because he sees God in all created things and all created things in God: he sees the One in All and All in One, but he can only love the universe because it is 'universal', not particular: the 'particular' person, simply because he claims to be a person in his own right, offends. The mystic is centred in God and knows that he is so centred, but so for that matter is the 'other'. The difference is that the 'other' does not know because he confuses his ephemeral ego with his immortal self, his *ahaṁkāra* with the *ātman*. He is still in what Aurobindo calls the 'Ignorance', but the same must be true of Teilhard too, for if he cannot see the Eternal in others he cannot truly know Christ as the Centre to which all apparently separate centres must, according to his own theory, aspire: hence he cannot love them, and his love of God must therefore be incomplete, or, as St. John would say, it is a lie.

Perhaps it is true to say that all mystics are born before their time: they see in eternity as God sees, but they do not realize that until this vision is generalized throughout mankind, their own vision of All in One and One in All is meaningless and a lie to all who do not so see. For we live in time, in evolutionary time, and we ourselves, as Teilhard himself saw as clearly as anyone else, are not static entities but parts of a *process*; indeed we are micro-processes ourselves, proceeding and ascending from the pure multiplicity of primal matter towards the pinnacle of spirit, what Teilhard calls Christ-Omega, the point into which the whole universe must converge. Only there can there be a universal mystical life in which death will be conquered and 'God will be all in all'[38].

In *The Phenomenon of Man* Teilhard, assuming that energy is the basis of all evolution, makes a distinction between what he calls 'tangential' and 'radial' energy, the first applying to the 'without' of things, the subject-matter of the natural sciences, the second to the 'within', the sphere of psychology and religion. More precisely, in the words of Claude Cué-

[38] 1 Corinthians, 15. 28.

not[39]: 'tangential energy [is] the measurable energy of the physicists in the domain of material reactions [while] radial or centric energy [is] the domain of the imponderable actions of arrangement and union—psychic energy which is released in proportion to the complexity of matter and which, grafting itself on the first, purely mechanical, "arrangements", directs animated matter towards higher and higher syntheses.' It is, then, 'radial' energy (which in his earlier works Teilhard is content to call spirit) that is responsible for what Engels calls 'qualitative leaps' and Teilhard the 'critical points' in evolution—notably the appearance of life out of apparently dead matter, and the appearance of consciousness out of life.

Each of these 'leaps' is definitive and cannot be reversed. But evolution does not move in a straight line. Always and everywhere and at all levels the forward thrust is thwarted by a *vis inertiae* which seeks to retard it. The thrust towards increased complexity and consciousness is always impeded and counterbalanced by a corresponding increase in entropy. Matter in itself is pure multiplicity and left to itself it will always revert to its original condition. 'Radial energy', on the other hand, which religion calls 'spirit' is the dynamic search for new, higher, more complex, more conscious, and more organized and unified forms of life: as Teilhard says, 'To create is to unite.' This is true as much on the collective level as on the individual. On the individual level the human brain is the most highly organized, complex, and integrated 'molecule' that evolution has yet developed. But though it may be true that, as Teilhard says, 'to think, one must eat', this does not explain anything, for the same food may be transformed into the drivellings of an idiot or into the epochmaking discoveries of a Newton or an Einstein. This is the work of 'radial energy' which science has found no means of assessing, any more than it has of explaining the 'qualitative leaps' of evolution.

[39] Claude Cuénot, *Teilhard de Chardin*, E.T., London, Burns and Oates, 1965, p. 352.

We have no means of knowing how the new phenomena of life and of what R. M. Bucke called simple consciousness were hampered and thwarted by the *vis inertiae* of 'pure' matter. Nor in the history of the human race can we do more than guess from mythology how men reacted when they first became self-conscious. That this was extremely painful and difficult to adjust to seems certain; for a 'qualitative leap' or 'critical point' is like a birth—a quite new form of existence issuing from the old; and the process must involve suffering as well as wastage. Since the rise of self-consciousness there have been pointers throughout the globe that sooner or later beyond full personal consciousness there is and must be a larger form of consciousness, a consciousness that is in some sense collective because shared by all. The pointers to this are, of course, the mystics whose experiences, despite the varieties among them, point unanimously to the destruction or at least the suppression of the ego, or to its fusion in the totality of things. This has been the constant theme of Indian religion, both Hindu and Buddhist. In early Buddhism indeed it is emphasized at the expense of everything else. Of nothing may you say, 'This is I,' 'This is mine,' 'This is the self,' or 'This belongs to the self.' This is the only way to peace and the only escape from suffering: it is a heroic severing of spirit from matter, a final rejection of the whole world of becoming and of the irreversible march of evolution, a refusal of our human condition as such and of any possibility of further development. And yet it is right in this sense that without withdrawal from the temporal there can be no contact with the eternal, without death there can be no resurrection, or in the terms of the Christian sacramental system, there can be no communion without first being baptized 'in death'[40]. For Theravāda Buddhism this is the end, but for the Mahāyāna it is a new beginning, the realization that we are no longer ourselves but participants in the eternal and transcendental Buddha-nature. But these are pointers only, pointers vouchsafed to individuals in anticipation of their extension to all mankind or rather that portion of mankind

[40] Romans, 6. 3.

which will consent to take the plunge into a death which is yet eternal life. Cosmic consciousness, says R. M. Bucke who invented the term, appearing in individuals, is the guarantee of a future cosmic consciousness that must one day be born and which will mean the transformation of the human race and its unification in and around a central focus of attraction, the *Sac-cid-ānanda* of Aurobindo, the Christ-Omega of Teilhard de Chardin. This evolutionary drive from simple consciousness to cosmic consciousness has been admirably sketched out by Bucke himself.

There is a tradition [he writes] probably very old, to the effect that the first man was innocent and happy until he ate of the fruit of the tree of the knowledge of good and evil. That having eaten thereof he became aware that he was naked and was ashamed. Further, that then sin was born into the world, the miserable sense whereof replaced man's former feeling of innocency. That then and not till then man began to labor and to cover his body. Stranger than all (so it seems to us), the story runs, that along with this change or immediately following upon it there came into man's mind the remarkable conviction which has never since left it but which has been kept alive by its own inherent vitality and by the teaching of all true seers, prophets and poets that this accursed thing which has bitten man's heel (laming him, hindering his progress and especially making this halting and painful) should eventually be crushed and subjugated by man himself—by the rising up within him of a Saviour—the Christ.

Man's progenitor was a creature (an animal) walking erect but with simple consciousness merely. He was (as are to-day the animals) incapable . . . of shame (at least in the human sense). He had no feeling or knowledge of good and evil. He as yet knew nothing of what we call work and had never labored. From this state he fell (or rose) into self consciousness, his eyes were opened, he knew that he was naked, he felt shame, acquired the sense of sin . . . , and learned to do certain things in order to encompass certain ends—that is, he learned to labor.

For weary eons this condition has lasted—the sense of sin still haunts his pathway—by the sweat of his brow he still eats bread—he is still ashamed. Where is the deliverer, the Saviour? Who or what?

The Saviour of man is Cosmic Consciousness—in Paul's language—the Christ. The cosmic sense (in whatever mind it appears) crushes the serpent's head—destroys sin, shame, the sense of good and evil as contrasted one with the other, and will annihilate labor, though not human activity.[41]

This is certainly as visionary as anything that either Aurobindo or Teilhard ever wrote; but the conclusion is surely false. Leaving aside 'sin, shame, and the sense of good and evil' for the moment, it is plainly absurd to say that cosmic consciousness will annihilate labour; nor is it at all evident that the march of evolution will be accompanied by an increase in the occurrence of cosmic consciousness. What is quite plain, however, is that labour will in fact be annihilated not by cosmic consciousness but by the creative upsurge of an all-conquering science. As even Aurobindo saw and as Teilhard never tired of repeating, in the modern world science and scientific research, alone among human activities, can unify the world externally because they create ever larger units co-operating voluntarily and purposefully in stupendous enterprises, the ever accelerating progress of which cannot but fire the imagination because there seems to be no end to the possibilities now open to man. Of course there have been casualties on the way as there must be if any 'qualitative leap' is to be achieved, but the death of the individual in the interest of the advancement of the species is at its lowest, as Teilhard says, 'the price paid by the parts for the progress and triumph of the whole. They are soldiers who have fallen on the field of honour.'[42] At its best it is 'a sort of breaking-up and recasting of our whole being, the condition for [our] recreation and integration into the Pleroma'[43].

In *The Phenomenon of Man* Teilhard had hailed science as the great principle of unity in the modern world:

[41] R. M. Bucke, *Cosmic Consciousness*, New York, Dutton, 1901 and reprints, pp. 6–7.
[42] *Oeuvres* 6, p. 63.
[43] In Christopher F. Mooney, S.J., *Teilhard de Chardin and the Mystery of Christ*, New York, Harper and Row, 1964, p. 116.

Through the discovery yesterday of the railway, the motor-car and the aeroplane, the physical influence of each man, formerly restricted to a few miles, now extends to hundreds of leagues or more. Better still: thanks to the prodigious biological event represented by the discovery of electro-magnetic waves, each individual finds himself henceforth (actively and passively) simultaneously present, over land and sea, in every corner of the earth.[44]

This was written in 1940. How childish it sounds today! Now, thanks to the team-work of four hundred thousand men, each dedicating his individual skill to a single enterprise, the conquest of the moon, man has at last broken physically out of this planet to conquer new worlds. And this is only made possible by the concentration of every type of scientific research and technological skill upon a single project—the centration of four hundred thousand human centres on a purely scientific centre which, being material, contains within it 'the combined essence of all evil and all good'.[45] The evil consequences that the inexorable advance of science might produce Teilhard was all too ready to discount. Of the splitting of the atom and the explosion of the first atomic bomb he could say:

The greatest discovery ever made by man was precisely the one in which for the first time the largest number of minds were able to join together in a single organism, both more complicated and more centred, for the purpose of research. Coincidence, you will say. No, should we not rather say that here as in other fields it was proved that nothing in the universe can hold out against the convergent enthusiasm of a large enough number of minds satisfactorily grouped and organized.[46]

Thus if the mystics have realized infinity within themselves, the scientists are now at last beginning to chart infinity without. At last we can begin to understand what the Upanishad meant when it spoke of 'the Self within the heart, smaller than a grain of rice or a barley-corn, or a mustard seed, or a grain of millet, or the kernel of a grain of millet,'

[44] The Phenomenon of Man, E.T., p. 240.   [45] Above, p. 21.
[46] Oeuvres 5, p. 183: E.T., The Future of Man, 1964, p. 144.

and of how this infinitesimal something is at the same time 'greater than the earth, greater than the atmosphere, greater than the sky, greater than all these worlds.'[47] 'This is what you must seek out, this is what you must want to understand.'[48]

So too is it now far easier to understand Teilhard when he said: 'Neither in its impetus nor in its achievements can science go to its limits without becoming tinged with mysticism and charged with faith.'[49] Even the scientists themselves are beginning to understand.

And in honour of the occasion the Pope, speaking a language that both Teilhard and Aurobindo would have approved, said: 'This very bold enterprise obliges us to look on high, beyond this earthly field, to remember the immense and serious reality in which our little life unfolds. This new discovery of created life is very important for our spiritual life. To see God in the world and the world in God, what is more exciting? Is it not thus that we escape the terror of the void that unmeasured time and unconfined space produce around the microcosm that is us?'[50]

True, man has now launched out into that which is 'greater than the great, greater than the earth, greater than the atmosphere, greater than the sky, greater than all these worlds'; and the whole universe of matter, not just this tiny planet of ours, seems now to be within his reach. He is in a position to bring the kingdom of heaven to earth, but is he in a position to universalize the kingdom of God within himself?

The conquest of matter is awesome; for matter is power, 'the combined essence of all evil and all good', and man has the power to use it for either, as we all know. And we also know both from the Upanishads and from Aurobindo that cosmic consciousness, the reflexion of the totality of matter within us, can also destroy the distinction between good and

---

[47] *Chāndogya* Upanishad, 3. 14. 4.   [48] Ibid., 8. 7. 1.
[49] *The Phenomenon of Man*, E.T., p. 284.
[50] Quoted in the *Tablet*, 26. 7. 69.

evil. 'He who has seen me once can never more forget me,' says Matter personified in Teilhard's parable entitled *The Spiritual Power of Matter*: 'either he damns himself with me, or he saves me with himself.'[51] So too with cosmic consciousness 'everything seems to come to life, but in reality everything is materialized'[52] and therefore morally neutral. Everything, then, so far from being centred on a pole of attraction ahead, is diffused in the oneness of pure multiplicity—primal matter without form or content and yet somehow suffused by the veiled and hidden Spirit of which Aurobindo speaks and which has yet to taste of the fruit of the tree of the knowledge of good and evil. Cosmic consciousness on its own is nothing; but when spiritualized by the fire of love it could and we can but hope that it will one day heal and weld together, 'moralize' and 'amorize', as Teilhard not very happily puts it, the human mass into one body and one soul. Today the reverse of what Christ said to his disciples in Gethsemane seems to be true. No longer is it true that 'the spirit is willing, but the flesh is weak'. Must we not rather say: 'Matter is willing, but the spirit is weak'? So let Matter be allowed to speak for herself once more in the words of Teilhard de Chardin:

You called me: here I am. Driven by the Spirit far from the path on which the human caravan travels, you dared to venture into an immaculate solitude. Grown weary of abstractions, of attenuations, of the wordiness of social life, you wanted to pit yourself against Reality, entire and untamed.

You needed me in order to grow; and I was waiting for you so that you might sanctify me.

Always you have desired me though you did not know it, and I have been drawing you on.

And now I am on you, for life or for death. You cannot go back, you cannot return to your everyday comforts and your untroubled worship. Once you have seen me, you can never forget me: you must either be damned with me, or I shall be saved with you.

[51] *Écrits du temps de la guerre*, p. 438: E.T. in *Hymn of the Universe*, 1965, p. 61.
[52] Above p. 20.

Are you coming?

'O you who are godlike and mighty, what is your name?' ...

I am the fire that consumes and the water that overthrows; I am the love that initiates and the truth that passes away. All that compels acceptance and all that brings renewal, all that breaks apart and all that unites—power, experience, progress—matter: all this am I.

Because of my violence I often kill my lovers; because he who touches me never knows what power he is unleashing, the wise fear me and curse me. They speak of me with scorn, calling me beggar-woman or witch or harlot. But their words are at variance with life, and the Pharisees who condemn me waste away in the spirit to which they restrict themselves. They die of inanition, and their disciples desert them because I am the essence of all that is tangible, and men cannot do without me.

You who have grasped that the world—the world beloved by God—has, even more than individuals, a soul to be redeemed, lay your whole being wide open to my inspiration, and receive the spirit of the earth which must be saved.

The last word of the enigma, the dazzling utterance which is inscribed on my brow and which will henceforth burn into your eyes if you close them is this: *Nothing is precious save what is yourself in others and others in yourself. In heaven all is but one. In heaven all is but one.*[53]

But the earth is still full of strife and hatred, discord, tyranny, envy, selfishness, and greed: for it is thus that we and our master, Satan, have built the city of God on earth.

---

[53] *Écrits du temps de la guerre*, pp. 438–9: E.T. in *Hymn of the Universe*, pp. 60–62.

III

THE COMMUNION OF SAINTS

'IN heaven all is but one. In heaven all is but one.' But Aurobindo said: 'Heaven we have possessed, but not the earth'.[1] This is the experience of the mystic: the opposite experience, that of 'possessing the earth', and not only the earth but the moon, the planets, and heaven knows what beyond, is already within the grasp of science—collective science which is fast becoming the common patrimony of mankind. On the one hand, then, you have heaven, the realm of spirit where all is but one, on the other you have the earth organizing itself at first through the mysterious power of evolution and then being consciously organized in these 'last days' by scientific man. Together they point to the Parousia: separated they constitute an unbridgeable dualism which it becomes ever more difficult to accept. Hence Aurobindo added: 'the fullness of the Yoga is to make . . . Heaven and earth equal and one.' What, then, is the link between them. In China it is man, in the Book of Genesis it is God.

In the beginning God created the heavens and the earth.

Who or what is 'God'? A Person certainly who wills and transforms his will into act, the author of *karma*, then, as in the Bhagavad-Gītā, but essentially separate from 'the heavens and the earth'—God, transcendent and One, Allah, the God of the Muslims:

Say: he is God, One,
God, the Eternal:
He did not beget, nor was he begotten,
And equal to him there has never been anyone, no, not one.[2]

[1] Above p. 8.   [2] Koran, 112.

But in the Hebrew the form is *Elohim*, grammatically a plural form, 'the gods', just as Persian *Yazdān* is a plural form from *Yazd* (*Izad*), for as the Upanishads say: 'The gods, it seems, love the obscure and hate the obvious.'[3]

God is One: on this the higher religions are in some degree united: but in Christianity he is also three, and this is a mystery which the Christians themselves have never been able to explain. And yet this Christian Trinity is reflected in Hindu theology too, not in the highly artificial trinity of Brahmā, the creator, Vishnu, the preserver, and Śiva, the destroyer, which is not comparable to the Christian Trinity at all, but in the standard Vedāntin formula *sac-cid-ānanda* which all Vedāntins and not least Aurobindo accept, Being–Consciousness–Joy, or without stretching the formula too much, Being–Logos–Love. The parallel is striking and we shall have to return to it. But to return now to that ever-fascinating first chapter of Genesis.

In the beginning God created the heavens and the earth. Now the earth was a formless void, there was darkness over the deep, and God's spirit hovered over the water.

We hear no more about the heavens, as is proper, for, as Teilhard says, 'in heaven all is but one'. But the earth is very different; it is *tohu* and *bohu*, a 'trackless waste and emptiness', dark and fluid, having no shape or form, coherence or consistency. Call it 'nothing' or 'no thing', say with 2 Maccabees (7.28) that 'God made them out of things that did not exist (ἐξ οὐκ ὄντων)': it doesn't matter very much since even the theologians are not very clear as to what creation *ex nihilo* means. Teilhard did his best to describe the 'nothing' from which God created the earth, and his account which tries to square evolution with Genesis rather than the dogmatic creation *ex nihilo* is intriguing if not very convincing to the rational mind. But then the rational mind is a 'peeper into key-holes',[4] always trying to explain away

---

[3] *Brihadāranyaka* Upanishad, 4. 2. 2.
[4] Cf. R. C. Zaehner, *The Bhagavad-Gītā*, Oxford, Clarendon Press, 1968, p. 176.

what cannot be explained: for Aurobindo it is indeed the fountain-head of Ignorance. This is how Teilhard put it in one of his earlier works:

In the beginning there were, at the two poles of existence, God and pure multiplicity (*la Multitude*). Even so God was all alone, because this pure multiplicity which was in a state of absolute dissociation did not exist. For all eternity God saw the shadow of his unity in a diffused state of disarray (*éparpillée*) beneath his feet; and this shadow, fraught as it was with every possibility of producing something, was not another God because, in itself, it did not exist, nor had it ever existed, nor could it ever have existed because its essence was to be infinitely divided in itself, that is to say, to tend towards nothingness. Infinite in extension, infinitely rarified, this pure multiplicity, annihilated as to its essence, slept at the antipodes of Being which is One and concentrated.

It was then that Unity, overflowing with life, joined battle through [the process of] creation with the multiple which, though non-existent [in itself] opposed it as a contrast and a challenge. To create, as it appears to me, means to condense, concentrate, organize, unite.[5]

'God was all alone,' Teilhard says. But how could he be alone if, as the Christians (and the Vedāntins) will have it he is a Trinity? And what was his 'Spirit' which hovered over the water? It can scarcely be other than the Holy Spirit commonly accounted as being the third 'Person' of the Christian Trinity. It 'hovered over the water' and, presumably, entered into the water—water, the symbol of the ever-moving, the unstable, perpetually changing thing which is chaos—matter in its most embryonic and, if you like, its most non-existent form. The Spirit, the principle of unity in the Godhead since it eternally binds the Father to the Son, descends into matter, descends into the dead, dark waters. Or as the Rig-Veda (10.129.3) puts it:

In the beginning was darkness swathed in darkness;
All was but unmanifested water.

[5] *Écrits du temps de la guerre*, p. 114: E.T. in *Writings in Time of War*, p. 95.

Whatever was, that One, coming into being,
Hidden by the Void,
Was generated by the power of heat.

'Hidden by the Void': this is essential in the thought of Aurobindo. Spirit or, as he more often calls it, Consciousness-Force descends into matter and there becomes veiled and alienated from itself. Though remaining in eternity unfettered and free in the triune Godhead it, so to speak, loses itself in the dark, dead waters of matter, but in so doing it stirs them into life.

Of Christ St. Paul wrote:

His state was divine,
yet he did not cling
to his equality with God
but emptied himself
to assume the condition of a slave,
and became as men are.[6]

This is the self-emptying of him who was styled the Son of God. Surely it is not fanciful to see just such a self-emptying of the Spirit of God at the time of creation? St. John says in his first Epistle (3.9):

No one who has been begotten by God sins;
because God's seed remains inside him,
he cannot sin when he has been begotten by God.

So too the Holy Spirit, the 'seed' of God, enters into matter —discontinuous, disjointed, incoherent matter so that in the course of millions of years she may give birth to man. Matter in herself is neither good nor evil; she is neutral, or rather she is, in Teilhard's words, the 'combined essence of all evil and all good'. In Hindu terminology she is both the *māyā* that conceals and the *māyā* that must one day unveil Spirit who has come to lodge within her. She is Mother Nature, the womb of all the worlds. For does not Krishna in the Gītā (14.3–4) also say:

---

[6] Philippians, 2. 6–7.

Great Nature[7] is to me a womb, in it I plant the seed; from this derives the origin of all contingent beings. . . . Great Nature is the womb, I the Father, giver of the seed.

God, the Father, then, on the one side; Nature, that is, Matter, the Mother of all material things on the other; and between them 'God's Spirit hovering over the water' to fertilize it and bring it to life. In the Gītā the union of God with material Nature is conceived of in purely sexual terms, and it is more than possible that an original pagan myth of which the first chapter of Genesis may be a monotheistic adaptation, told the same tale: God consorts with Matter that Matter may be quickened with new life: the 'seed'— the Spirit—dies that in due course man may be born, spiritual on his Father's side, material on his mother's.

This may sound fanciful to modern Christian ears, but I doubt whether it would sound at all fanciful to a Hindu; for in the Gītā God is both 'the Father, giver of the seed' and the seed itself 'that does not pass away' (9.18). This is the Holy Spirit that descended into the 'waters' of matter before time began: it is the first 'baptism', the fruit of which will be the first man. The 'waters' of matter are fertilized by the 'seed' of Spirit, just as the baptismal water is fertilized by the same Spirit in the blessing of the font in the old Holy Saturday liturgy of the Catholic Church. The idea is the same: in each case the 'seed' 'dies' in the female element—Spirit dies in matter—in order to be reborn as man, in the one case Adam, the 'All-man', as Julian of Norwich calls him, in the second case the 'New Man', Jesus Christ, the 'twice-born' of the Hindu tradition.

You have been taught that when we were baptized in Christ Jesus we were baptized in his death.[8]

And so, just as Christ dies that new life may be born, so, at the beginning of time, does the Spirit 'die' so that the

---

[7] *Brahma* exceptionally used in the sense of 'material Nature'. See R. C. Zaehner, op. cit., p. 352.

[8] Romans, 6. 3.

human race may be born. In the old liturgy of Holy Saturday the symbolism is patently, almost embarassingly, sexual. The Paschal candle is thrice plunged into the water, penetrating into it deeper each time. During each dipping the priest says: *Descendat in hanc plenitudinem fontis virtus Spiritus Sancti*—'May the vigour (one might almost translate "manhood" in accordance with the etymology) of the Holy Spirit descend into the fulness (*plenitudo* = πλήρωμα) of this fount.' And after the third dipping 'breathing thrice upon the water in the form of the Greek letter Ψ he goes on: *Totamque hujus aquae substantiam regenerandi foecundet effectu,*— "and may he make the whole substance of this water fruitful for the purpose of regeneration."' The symbolism of both action and words is unmistakable: the Paschal candle representing the 'manhood' of the Holy Spirit is the *lingam* and the font is the *yoni*—*Purusha* and *Prakriti*, Śiva and his Śakti. The symbol of their union is the Greek letter Ψ, an almost perfect representation of the union of the male and female generative organs. There is nothing shocking in this, for not only has the union of the sexes been a constant symbol for the act of creation, but even in Christianity what is considered to be the most perfect symbol of the soul's union with God is the spiritual *marriage*, and the Church too is described as the *bride* of Christ. So too creation is the 'marriage' of God the Father with Matter, and the Spirit, as in the Gītā, is his 'seed'. This means that matter is both fertilized and sanctified, the perishable is united with the Imperishable, and the fruit of the union is man. In the second, Yahwistic account of creation the metaphor changes.

Yahweh God fashioned man of dust from the soil. Then he breathed into his nostrils a breath of life, and thus man became a living being.[9]

The breath of life is, of course, the same 'breath', the same 'Spirit', 'that hovered over the water' and fertilized it. As such it is the *creator Spiritus*, the creative Spirit, that indwells

[9] Genesis, 2. 7.

the whole evolutionary process, 'veiled' and hidden in matter as Aurobindo would say, but driving it ever onwards to life and consciousness. For this a second 'descent' of the Holy Spirit was required: a barely conscious brute had to be transmuted into a living and conscious being. Hence man receives a new 'breath of life' which the Hindus call *prāna*; and as the *Kaushītakī* Upanishad says (3.3,4): 'What the breath of life is, that is consciousness: what consciousness is, that is the breath of life. For both of them dwell together in this body, and together they depart.'

Let us pause for a moment to consider the nature of man in Genesis as it may be interpreted in the light of evolution. There are two accounts, the one emanating from what is conventionally called the 'priestly' tradition, the other from the 'Yahwistic'. In the first, matter is impregnated by God's Spirit as seed. This endows it with physical life. In the second, *man* appears as a living and conscious being made aware of himself by God's Spirit as breath: he is an uneasy amalgam of the material and the divine, of *Prakriti* and *Purusha*, the perishable and the immortal. In the priestly account, however, man emerges not as just the highest of the animals but made in the image and likeness of God: he must then share in the divine nature as it is in eternity; he is a material being that nevertheless shares in the changeless essence of God and in his creative power, 'little less than a god', 'crowned with glory and splendour', and 'lord over the work of [God's] hands'[10]. Yet, however true this may be of man in his full development, it can scarcely have been true of him as he emerged from simple consciousness into full self-consciousness, coming to know good and evil.

In the beginning, then, Spirit descended into matter, emptied itself, lost itself, was 'veiled' to itself, unaware of itself. This means that there is no such thing as really 'dead' matter; all matter is instinct with life and consciousness. What Teilhard calls the 'Soul of the world' and Aurobindo

[10] Psalm 8. 5–6.

calls 'Supermind' is already there in embryo, just as the soul of an individual is already there, though unconscious, in the human foetus. It is there but it has not yet developed; yet it develops slowly but inexorably until we arrive at the simple consciousness of the animal, and then in the first human beings or rather groups of human beings at a kind of collective consciousness which seems to precede full self-consciousness. For, as Teilhard says, 'in the opinion of the best observers a kind of collective co-consciousness can still be distinguished among tribes classified by ethnologists as primitive which in the most natural way in the world enables the group to stick together and to function harmoniously as a group.'[11] This is a primitive form of cosmic consciousness, the shared collective consciousness of primitive human society which the Bible calls Adam. At this stage of his development man was innocent as the animals are innocent because he still followed the law that Nature had assigned to him and before the hidden Spirit had pushed him forward into full self-consciousness, individual responsibility, and a knowledge of good and evil. Living in and with and by the collective consciousness of the group the individual was not conscious of life and death, for though an individual, he had no consciousness of individuality, he had not yet learnt to say 'I'. This was the state of the All-man, Adam, as it was the state of his Chinese counterpart, the True Man of the Taoist philosopher Chuang Tze:

The True Man of ancient times knew nothing of loving life, knew nothing of hating death. He emerged without delight; he went back in without a fuss. He came briskly, he went briskly, and that was all. He didn't forget where he began; he didn't try to find out where he would end. He received something and took pleasure in it; he forgot about it and handed it back again. This is what I call not using the mind to repel the Way, not using man to help out Heaven. This is what I call the True Man. . . . Therefore his liking was one and his not liking was one. His being one and his not being one was one. In being one, he was acting as a

[11] Teilhard, *Oeuvres* 8, p. 135: cf. E.T. *Man's Place in Nature*, p. 93.

companion of Heaven. In not being one, he was acting as a companion of man. When man and Heaven do not defeat each other, then he may be said to have the True Man.[12]

This, we must suppose, was the state of Adam and Eve in the garden of Eden, of primitive mankind, that is, in its first stage of co-consciousness. Individual death meant nothing to him, for he lived not with his own life but with that of the species: herein lay his immortality. He was not an angel but a very small child. And just as nothing can prevent a child from growing up into a responsible human being unless he is mentally handicapped, so nothing could prevent the human race from growing up out of a state of co-consciousness into a state of full self-consciousness: like the individual the race too had to grow up. Why, then, did the Lord God say to these innocents: 'You may eat indeed of all the trees in the garden. Nevertheless of the tree of the knowledge of good and evil you are not to eat, for on the day you eat of it you shall most surely die.'[13] Could he really have wished the human race to remain in a state of collective ignorance, however blissful this might be? Perhaps, for in the first two chapters of Genesis God himself is not an integrated personality; for the 'total' God is not only Yahweh, the heavenly Father, but also the serpent, the Spirit of the Earth, hidden in the waters of matter and struggling to break out into a wider freedom. This is not wholly fanciful, for the serpent is an ambivalent being in the Bible, and Jesus himself had bidden his disciples to 'be as subtle as serpents and gentle as doves'. Could he have been referring to two opposing aspects of the Holy Spirit? Be that as it may,

The serpent was the most subtle of all the wild beasts that Yahweh God had made. It asked the woman, 'Did God really say you were not to eat from any of the trees in the garden?' The woman answered the serpent, 'We may eat the fruit of the trees

[12] Chuang Tze, 6. 2: see Burton Watson, *Chuang Tzu, Basic Writings*, New York and London, Columbia University Press, 1964, pp. 74–6.

[13] Genesis 2. 16–7.

in the garden. But of the fruit of the tree in the middle of the garden God said, "You must not eat it, nor touch it, under pain of death".' Then the serpent said to the woman, 'No! You will not die! God knows in fact that on the day you eat it your eyes will be opened and you will be like gods, knowing good and evil.'[14]

We all know the sequel. They ate of the fruit and their eyes were opened. When in a state of co-consciousness in which the individual lived with the life of the whole, they 'knew nothing of loving life, nothing of hating death', for they did not know that they must die. Once their eyes were opened to the knowledge of good and evil, however, 'they realized that they were naked', that is, that they were defenceless in a hostile world, and that everywhere death lay in wait for them. They knew that they must die.

This is the price of individual consciousness, the price we have to pay for the birth of mind, ignorant as yet, as Aurobindo would say, that there is such a thing as Supermind. In a sense it is a Fall, for man has now lost his sense of solidarity with the cosmos; but in a sense it is a rise, for he has discovered himself as man, as an evolving creature with limitless possibilities, 'little less than a god', 'crowned with glory and splendour', and 'lord of the work of [God's] hands'. But the price he has paid is that each individual must from now on make himself the centre of his own universe: man has learnt to say 'I', and having learnt to say 'I', it could only have been a question of time before he would come to say 'mine' too. Egoism, the root-sin of mankind, was born.

What, then, is the position of 'fallen' man as it is revealed to us in the more ancient religions of the world? Let us take the Hebrews first, for it is with them that we began. The price man has to pay for yielding to what seemed to be the sweetly reasonable blandishments of the serpent, the Spirit of the Earth, is not only that he now knows that as an individual he must die. He also finds himself pitted not only against animals physically stronger than himself but also

[14] Ibid., 3. 1–5.

against his fellow-men and against a God who appears to be both capricious and unjust. The image of God in man has been shattered, and God is determined that it shall not be restored except on his own incomprehensible terms. He shows himself not as a friend but as 'a bully and a tyrant'[15]. For no reason at all he accepts Abel's sacrifice but rejects the sacrifice of Cain; or is it because Cain, the tiller of the soil, represents a more advanced stage of civilization than does Abel, the shepherd who keeps flocks? By his own injustice Yahweh sows the seeds of dissension between the brothers, and Cain slays Abel—an ominous prelude enough, one would have thought, to the humanist ideal of the brotherhood of man. For the ancient Hebrew, then, the Fall meant not only the severing of man's links with God, but also of what had hitherto been his link with his fellow-men. Co-consciousness has gone, and man has not yet learnt how to organize himself on the basis of individual self-consciousness. This Yahweh is determined he shall not do except in blind obedience to himself. The serpent had promised that by eating the fruit of the tree of the knowledge of good and evil men would become 'like gods'; but if, as now seemed likely, they were to be perpetually at war with one another, how could they recapture the godlike quality of unity and union in a common consciousness which they had enjoyed before the Fall? The story is told in the myth of the Tower of Babel. Mankind, now scattered, though still speaking one language, decides to come together and unite in one single great city.

'Come,' they said, 'let us build ourselves a town and a tower with its top reaching heaven. Let us make a name for ourselves, so that we may not be scattered about the whole earth,

Now Yahweh came down to see the town and the tower that the sons of man had built. 'So they are all a single people with a single language!' said Yahweh. 'This is but the start of their undertakings! There will be nothing too hard for them to do. Come, let us go down and confuse their language on the spot so

[15] Above, p. 38.

that they can no longer understand one another. Yahweh scattered them thence over the whole face of the earth, and they stopped building the town.[16]

This, in the Hebrew account, is man's first attempt to unite of his own accord, the first rationalist and humanist endeavour to establish a united and ordered society without reference to the divine. The divine, however, in the shape of Yahweh, is also a suppressed content of the human unconscious: he is the irrational power that perpetually thwarts man in his efforts to perfect himself both individually and collectively in accordance with what he conceives to be the dictates of reason. For if man is subject to evolution, so too is God, or at least the idea of God as it develops in man's mind. In the Old Testament there is no clear distinction between God and the Devil any more than there is in Hinduism. Yahweh, like the Indra of the *Kaushītakī* Upanishad, is violently destructive because he is beyond good and evil. God demands that man should be moral, but he himself, like the 'liberated' self in Hinduism, is beyond justice and injustice, *dharma* and *adharma*. All he asks of man is obedience. If his image is to be restored to man, then it must be on his own terms—and they are peculiar.

For in what did the image of God consist? First of all man resembled God in that he was eternal: he was, to use the Sanskrit expression, *brahmabhūta*. Secondly, as the 'All-man', his members, the individuals who together made up his collective body, were in full and perfect harmony through the Spirit which was the bond between them. Let us see how the great Greek father, Gregory of Nyssa, conceived of this godlike state. God, he says,

did not make the heavens in his image, nor the moon, the sun, the beauty of the stars, nor anything else which you can see in the created universe. You alone are made in the likeness of that nature which surpasses all understanding; you alone are a similitude of eternal beauty, a receptacle of happiness, an image of the true light; and if you look up to him, you will become what he is,

[16] Genesis, 11. 4–8.

imitating him who shines within you, whose glory is reflected in your purity. Nothing in all creation can equal your grandeur. All the heavens can fit into the palm of God's hand; the earth and the sea are measured in the hollow of his hand. And though he is so great that he can grasp all creation in his palm, you can wholly embrace him; he dwells within you, nor is he cramped as he pervades your entire being. . . .

If you realize this you will not allow your eye to rest on anything of this world. Indeed, you will no longer marvel even at the heavens. For how can you admire the heavens . . . when you see that you are more permanent than they? For the heavens pass away, but you will abide for all eternity with him who is forever.[17]

In this state of original innocence God walked in the Garden with man, and man was suffused by his eternal Being. To love God, then, was to love himself in all beings and all beings in himself; and because the human phylum was as yet bound together by what Teilhard calls co-consciousness, he loved his neighbour as himself because through the Holy Spirit of God he *was* himself. Then came the Fall, precipitated, we venture to think, by the same Holy Spirit directing and pushing forward the evolutionary process. Man stands alone, naked and ashamed. How is he to regain paradise lost?

There would seem to be two ways—the way of India and the way of China. The way of India was the way of the *Katha* Upanishad (4.1):

A certain sage, in search of immortality,
Turned his eyes inward and saw the Self within.

This is the way of the individual, the way of the hermit— to rediscover the unity and the harmony of God and the universe within oneself; and so 'when once one understands that in oneself the Self has become all beings, when once one has seen the unity, what room is there for sorrow, what room for perplexity?'[18] This is to reconstruct the kingdom

[17] Gregory of Nyssa, *Commentarius in canticum canticorum, Oratio 2*, 807–8: E T. in Jean Daniélou S.J. *From Glory to Glory*, tr. Herbert Musurillo S.J., London, John Murray, 1962, pp. 162–3.

[18] *Iśā* Upanishad, 7.

of God within you, but to leave out of account altogether the city of God on earth. This was the way of the Taoists in China too: it was not the way of the Confucians. For the Confucian ideal was a social ideal. It was not enough to restore the cosmic unity in individual men: this was not the answer to the new phenomenon of individual self-consciousness and the new and irreversible situation it had created. The shattering of the old unity, the co-consciousness of the race, could not be restored; a new unity in which 'the free development of each would be the condition for the free development of all' had to be found. Man would have to constitute himself as a middle term between Heaven, his Father, and Earth, his Mother. Hence the Confucians saw in the ordered harmony of the Chinese Empire bound together in filial piety under the Emperor, the Son of Heaven, and in close communion with the Spirit of the Earth, a truly *human* restoration of the divine unity which had been present in the 'All-man' but which had been shattered by the emergence of individual 'egos' each claiming a personal independence and rejecting that interdependence which was the natural corollary of co-consciousness. This was the Confucian ideal, a *social* ideal built on the concept of a harmonious society held together by ritual and centred on the person of the Emperor, the Son of Heaven. Thus we have two solutions—the Indian, which concentrated on the kingdom of God within, and the Chinese, which sought to build the city of God on earth: an esoteric solution and an exoteric one, both seeking to re-establish the eternal order in time, the first 'within' and the second 'without'; in the one case the experience of timeless bliss within, in the other the establishment of an immortal and, so far as possible, unchanging harmony in the context of a social whole. Either solution would restore the shattered unity and thereby overcome individual death by eliminating the subject of death which is the ego. For both the death of the ego is of no importance—for the Indian because it is not the real man but a usurper who lays claim to being the centre and directing principle of the human psyche whereas the truth of the matter is that the true centre is not the ego at all but the self within you whose essential being is outside time and can therefore never die; and for the Chinese because the ego is (or is supposed to be) re-integrated into the imperial collective unity in which it must lose itself, thereby finding 'immortality' in the life of the whole. Hence for Confucius the whole idea of life after death was irrelevant.

So too in Israel. So far as the Jews had any idea of immortality at all, it was conceived of as that of the people, not of the individual. But even this is not important; for Judaism differs from both Indian and Chinese religion radically. Whereas both Indian and Chinese religion are primarily interested in restoring a lost equilibrium, a lost *samatvam*, which had characterized the dawn of humanity, Israel always looked *forward* to the eventual establishment of a just and perfect society under the direct rule of the 'Lord God of Israel' or of his chosen Messiah. Israel moves in history, and its whole religion is conditioned by the storms and stresses of history, and, quite unlike any other religion, it sees history in terms of suffering meted out to herself by an arbitrary God whose will she, from the point of view of purely human reason, quite justifiably flouts. Judaism is the religion of evolution, starting with the birth of individual self-consciousness, the Fall, and ending in the establishment of the city of God on earth. But Judaism, of all the religions, is also the most realistic. So far as it admits of an afterlife at all, it is the shadowy and miserable existence in the pit of Sheol, and its God is, as Aurobindo would put it, a 'bully and a tyrant'[19], a dreadful and apparently unco-ordinated amalgam of the Zoroastrian Ohrmazd and Ahriman—the Vedic Rudra, furious yet strangely kind. Such is Yahweh throughout most of the Old Testament; but in the Prophets we begin to learn that he is predominantly a God of love, and in the New Testament we are taught that his dark and terrible side is, though ultimately subject to him, his Advers-

[19] Above p. 38.

ary and the thwarter of all his works. For in the New Testament two new divine persons emerge before our eyes, two 'sons of God'[20]—Jesus who, like the Zoroastrian Ohrmazd, is all good, and Satan who, like the Zoroastrian Ahriman, is all evil.

For Christians, of course, the Incarnation is the central event in history; but this seems very odd, for the life and death of Jesus seem to have passed almost unnoticed in the outside world and the spread of Christianity was a relatively slow affair. How unlike the coming of Muhammad whose religion appeared in the full light of day, spread with the speed of lightning, overthrew the mighty Persian Empire and wrenched vast territories from the suzerainty of Rome. Why, then, this insistence on the centrality of Jesus Christ?

Seen objectively, Jesus is the founder of one of the three world religions which have withstood the test of time—the other two being, of course, Gautama the Buddha and Muhammad. Chronologically he stands midway between the other two. So too, one might say, does he ideologically: he is the middle point between 'the kingdom of God within us', the Nirvāna of the Buddhists, and 'the city of God on earth', the theocracy of the four 'orthodox' Caliphs which all Sunnī Muslims look back to as the only true Muslim society. He is also, in Christian theology, the mid-point between the Father and the Holy Spirit, the second and central Person of the three 'Persons' of the Holy Trinity.

Buddhism too considers itself to be the Middle Way, the middle way between excessive asceticism and self-indulgence; but Christ too is the 'middle' Way, Truth, and Light between the ways, truths, and lights of Buddhism and Islam, just as the Gītā, the only Hindu scripture in which God speaks in the first person, is the middle way between the absolute monism of the non-dualist Vedānta and the absolute dualism of the Sānkhya; and for an obvious reason, for in effect absolute monism is *in practice* identical with the absolute dualism of both Sānkhya and Theravāda Buddhism in that

[20] Cf. Job, i. 6.

it sees salvation solely in terms of spirit. Matter, whether it is regarded as being merely illusory or as having an independent existence of its own, is that which enslaves spirit and that from whose bondage release must be sought. The two cannot be brought together unless spirit enters deeply into matter and moulds it towards a higher and more unified form of existence. This is what the Gītā does, and in this it supplements and completes Christianity.

'To create,' says Teilhard, 'is to unite.' This is true up to a point, true at least on the purely physical plane; but is it also true on the plane of conscious evolution, that is to say, is it true of human history? The serpent—the Spirit of evolution in matter—presented Eve with a choice. It had not occurred to her before that it was possible to disobey a divine command; or, in more evolutionary terms, she had hitherto acted like the animals, entirely by instinct. Her instinct therefore told her that the 'tree of knowledge' bore poisoned fruit, but when, under the serpent's guidance, she 'saw that the tree was good to eat and pleasing to the eye, and that it was desirable for the knowledge that it could give, she took some of its fruit and ate it'[21] with the disastrous results we all know. But a new element had now entered into evolution, freedom of the will and the ability to choose between alternatives each of which has its own attractions. With man evolution is no longer automatic: an element has evolved from it which can either assist its drive towards unity or impede and obstruct it. The first result of the appearance of self-consciousness, however, is not to unite but to diversify; and diversity, more often than not, means discord. Hence the tension between Yahweh (the tender father who would keep his children from growing up in order to spare them the stresses of adolescence and adult responsibility) on the one hand and the serpent, the Spirit of the Earth, who bids him break through the barrier that prevents him from being fully himself and damn the consequences on the other. The immediate result is discord and war

[21] Genesis, 3. 6.

symbolized by the myth of Cain and Abel. For the Holy Spirit, in so far as he is the Spirit of the Earth, is as ambivalent as is Yahweh himself; for Yahweh is all tenderness so long as his children remain docile and obedient, but savagely vindictive when they try to grow up and set up house on their own. So too the Spirit of the Earth impels man towards self-consciousness without warning him that self-consciousness brings with it the seeds of discord, hatred, pride, fear, envy, avarice and all those purely human sins which are not of the flesh but of the Devil. With the murder of Abel Satan, that pure *spirit* of evil for the first time appears on the scene—Satan, the 'father of lies', the spirit whose essence is discord, disunion, egoism, and spiritual pride. If, then, there is something of the Holy Spirit in the serpent as depicted in Genesis, Christian tradition on its side is nonetheless right when it identifies it with the Devil, for the two spirits seem as yet to be fused in one. But a separation is inevitable, and once separated the conflict between the two makes the stuff of human history. Egoism is always countered by a will to unite, either freely or more often by force. If Satan is *der Geist der stets verneint*, the Holy Spirit is *der Geist der stets vereint*.

In the fullness of time this same Spirit entered into the womb of the Virgin Mary, and the new Man was born, Jesus 'God Saves', who is also Emmanuel, 'God among us'. Mary, then, is the 'matter' from which the new Man is born, just as the 'waters' of matter were the womb from which in the beginning the whole of creation sprang. But now there is a difference. In the first case Spirit enters into pure multiplicity in order to wield it together into ever more complex forms until matter, having evolved life, evolves simple consciousness and co-consciousness, and finally, on the prompting of the ambivalent serpent, it evolves self-consciousness in Adam, the 'All-man'. History has begun; and history is the story of individuals acting in aggregates. Man's natural tendency to unite is always thwarted by his equally natural tendency to go it alone. When he unites he is usually compelled to do so by egos more overmastering than are the more feeble egos of the herd. But evolution's goal is not this; rather it is, to quote Marx again, to bring about 'an association in which the free development of each will be the condition for the free development of all'. But such an association requires a centre to hold it together around which it can cohere. Hence the Holy Spirit's second descent into matter had to be into a single point. His first descent had been into the 'greater than the great' of the *Katha* Upanishad, his second was to be into the 'smaller than the small' in the shape of a 'lowly handmaid' espoused to a carpenter, the utterly insignificant 'matter' from which a new creation was to be born. As the Vedic hymn says:

> From [Man, *Purusha*] was Virāj born,
> From Virāj Man again:
> Once born—behind, before—
> He reached beyond the earth.[22]

In the Christian tradition, then, Mary is Virāj, offspring of the first man, Adam, and mother of the second, Jesus. She is *mater*, 'mother', but also *materia*, 'matter', what the Gītā calls God's 'higher material Nature developed into life by which this world is kept in being'[23]. As the 'matter' from which the new Man is to be born she is also *māyā*, just as Mahāmāyā, 'great Māyā', gives birth to the Buddha in the Buddhist story. Mary is sanctified matter, the mother of the Man who was also God because the 'seed' that made the Virgin's womb fruitful was the Holy Spirit.

Et homo factus est: 'And he was made man.' This is at the centre of the Christian mystery.

> His state was divine,
> yet he did not cling
> to his equality with God
> but emptied himself
> to assume the condition of a slave,
> and became as men are;

[22] Rig-Veda, 10. 90. 5.   [23] Bhagavad-Gītā, 7. 5.

and being as all men are,
he was humbler yet,
even to accepting death,
death on a cross.
But God raised him high
and gave him the name
which is above all other names
so that all beings
in the heavens, on earth and in the underworld,
should bend the knee at the name of Jesus
and that every tongue should acclaim
Jesus Christ as Lord,
to the glory of God the Father.[24]

We have something like this in the *Tao Tê Ching* too:

The Way that can be told is not the unvarying Way;
The names that can be named are not the unvarying names.
It was from the Nameless that Heaven and Earth sprang.[25]

The Word became flesh, and the Nameless received a name, Jesus, 'God Saves', and Emmanuel, 'God among us', yet lowly, 'humble' and a 'slave'.

Therefore the Sage
In order to be above the people
Must speak as though he were lower than the people.
In order to guide them
He must put himself behind them.
Only thus can the Sage be on top and the people not be
  crushed by his weight.
Only thus can he guide, and the people not be led into harm.[26]

So it was that the Tao, the 'Way' who is also the Truth and the Light, entered the world, humble and unperceived, born in a manger 'by the Holy Spirit of the Virgin Mary'— the Man who was to be the second All-man, destined to be the focus of all human matter that can be spiritualized and 'saved', the Superman, if you like, of both Aurobindo and Teilhard de Chardin. This Superman, however, is also the

---

[24] Philippians, 2. 6–11.   [25] *Tao Tê Ching*, 1.   [26] Ibid., 66.

man whom the Evangelicals proclaimed in India, the preacher of the Sermon on the Mount so well-loved of Mahatma Gandhi. But Christianity is not just the Sermon on the Mount which is quite as Buddhist as it is Christian; but the preacher, it was claimed, was also God, the Word, the second Person of the Holy Trinity, the *Cit* of the Sanskrit Trinitarian formula *sac-cid ānanda*, the principle of rationality and order through and in which the universe coheres and follows eternal and unchanging laws. Hence it was the second Person of the Holy Trinity, the Logos, who had to become incarnate since man, as Aurobindo says in a telling phrase, 'is an abnormal who has not found his own normality'[27], that is, his own Logos. The Logos (most misleadingly translated as Word) made man, therefore, is the purely human 'normality' of man presented to him both as a doctrine and, much more essentially, as a human *life*, lived in flagrant opposition to all the received standards of the 'world', standards dictated by all the egoisms, both individual and collective, that had accumulated since the 'Fall'. First as to the teaching: this consists not only of the self-giving preached in the Sermon on the Mount but also in the explicit and impassioned denunciation of all self-righteousness, whether overt or covert, which reaches its climax in that excoriating twenty-third chapter of St Matthew with its inexorable refrain: 'Woe unto you, scribes and Pharisees, *hypocrites*!' addressed to the religious establishment of the time, but addressed also to all the establishments, whether religious or secular, of all time. To say that we know nothing of the historical Jesus seems to me a bit of not very clever nonsense. The Jesus of the synoptics is as living a human being and as vital a one as is the man Paul who reveals himself in his letters, as real as and more so than Socrates or Confucius, Guru Nānak or Kabīr. Here we have a life which is the absolute antithesis of the kind of life the Jews expected from their Messiah, a life of humility and self-effacement, of absolute and deliberate rejection of all

[27] *The Human Cycle*, p. 315.

the accepted social norms and of cant and humbug in all their manifold disguises (for was he not the friend of tax-collectors and prostitutes?), of hardship, and finally in Gethsemane of spiritual anguish and near-despair. This is what we start with, not the cosmic Christ of St. Paul as developed by Teilhard de Chardin. This is 'the grain of wheat that must fall on the ground and die in order that it may yield a rich harvest'[28], the man, Jesus of Nazareth, son of Mary.

In the Gītā (4.8) Krishna, himself a God incarnate, says that the purpose of his becoming man was 'for the protection of the good, for the destruction of evil-doers, for the setting up of the law of righteousness.' But there was a further purpose and this is made explicit in the Catholic Mass where we read that God became man 'that we might be made partakers in the divinity of him who deigns to participate in our humanity'. God becomes man in order that man may become God. But you cannot become God until you become like the man who God became—Jesus, son of Mary. But if this were all there was to it, there would have been no Christianity, for it would leave out of account the institution of the Eucharist, the sacrificial death on the Cross, and the resurrection; for St. Paul is quite right when he says: 'If Christ has not been raised then our preaching is useless and your believing is useless.'[29] But before he died, Christ instituted the sacrament of unity, the *material* sacrament of his own body and blood mysteriously present in the consecrated bread and wine, the sacramental centre and focus of unity, the food that transforms our carnal body into a spiritual body[30] so that all might grow together into his mystical body which is the Church.

'Brahman is food:' 'Brahman is breath:' 'Brahman is mind:' 'Brahman is understanding:' 'Brahman is joy.'[31] This, in purely evolutionary terms, makes sense, and since

---

[28] Cf. John, 12. 24. [29] 1 Corinthians, 15. 14.
[30] Ibid., 15. 44. [31] *Taittirīya* Upanishad, 3. 2–6.

we are men, not angels, we ultimately rely on food, for, as Teilhard says, 'to think, we must eat'. Yet in the Christian context this passage from the *Taittirīya* Upanishad is extraordinarily significant, for it means that for the Christian, Brahman, the Eternal and the very principle of eternity, becomes our food in the rite of communion. And a Christian can very well understand the Upanishad when it says: 'Food should not be despised:' 'food should not be set at naught:' 'food should be multiplied,' as it was multiplied at the feeding of the five thousand, itself the figure of the Eucharist, of Christ as the bread of life'[32], 'that food that endures to eternal life'[33]. Surely it might have been the eucharistic Christ speaking in those extraordinary last verses of the *Taittirīya* Upanishad:

I am food! I am food! I am food!
I am an eater of food! I am an eater of food! I am an eater
    of food! . . .
I am the first-born of the universal order,
Earlier than the gods, in the navel of immortality!
Whoso gives me away, he, verily, has succoured me!
I who am food eat the eater of food!
I have overcome the whole world!

'I who am food eat the eater of food.' Christ in the Eucharist is our food, but in being consumed by us, he in turn transforms us into himself, into his resurrected and 'spiritual' body. We must diminish so that he may increase.

The sacrament has been instituted. There follows the sacrificial death on the Cross. This has sometimes been interpreted as meaning the death of the ego in the higher and eternal 'self'; but surely there is more to it than this. For on the Cross it was not only a man who died but a God. Not only did the *ahaṁkāra* perish but the *ātman* too, and this 'destruction of the self'[34] is, according to the Gītā, the 'triple gate of hell', the lot reserved for the very vilest of sinners. So too Christ was 'cursed for our sake'[35], and 'for

---

[32] John 6. 35ff.   [33] Ibid., 6. 27.
[34] Bhagavad-Gītā, 16. 21.   [35] Galations, 3. 13.

our sake' again 'God made the sinless one into sin, so that in him we might become the goodness of God'[36]. For our sake he had to suffer 'destruction of the self', the blotting out of his very godhead, the 'triple gate of hell'. The emptying was now complete, but this was the necessary new beginning.

Christ died and rose from the dead, now in very truth the Man-God, the Superman in Aurobindo's sense, for 'God had made this Jesus whom you crucified both Lord and Christ'[37]. But the resurrected and ascended Jesus is not just the Lord in heaven 'seated at the right hand of the Father', he is also the indwelling God, the life that lives in Paul[38], the 'Person' who is exalted beyond and above the principle of eternity itself which the Hindus call Atman-Brahman[39], the true centre of every creature both in its being and in its never-ending becoming, whose body 'born of the Virgin Mary by the Holy Spirit' lives on in the sacrament of the altar and in the Church of which 'we are the living parts'[40].

The total sacrifice, the total 'emptying' of everything, both human and divine, constitutes the new birth, the transformation of the man Jesus into the new All-man Christ, the second Adam. The difference between the two is that whereas the rise to self-consciousness in the first Adam led to the separation and scattering of the human race and to the loss of that primitive co-consciousness that had held the race together, the death and resurrection of Jesus is at the same time the birth of the new All-man whose body is both Sacrament and Church. He is both the innermost and death-less centre of every individual, the visible and tangible bread and wine which is his body and blood, and the exterior reality which is the Catholic Church. He is the King of the kingdom of heaven within us as well as of the city of God on earth. But the city of God on earth, the body of the new Adam, still needs to be quickened by the Spirit. It is as if the infant Church were holding its breath in rapt anticipation of the life-giving Spirit that was still to come.

[36] 2 Corinthians, 5. 21.   [37] Acts, 2. 36.   [38] Cf. Galatians, 2. 20.
[39] Cf. Gītā, 14. 27.   [40] Ephesians, 5. 30.

Of the first Adam it was written: 'God fashioned man of dust from the soil. Then he breathed into his nostrils the breath'—the Spirit—'of life, and thus man became a living being.' The first Adam is formed from particles of matter that have grown together and coalesced into a physical organism that is not yet quite human. So too the 'body' of the second Adam is made up of a nucleus of human beings including Mary, his mother[41], the material element from which the man Jesus was drawn; but though united in their faith in the resurrected Lord, they are still primarily individuals and they do not know that it is they who form the terrestrial body of the risen Lord. It needed a further outpouring of the Holy Spirit to infuse a new spiritual and collective life into them by which a new Tower of Babel might be built, but this time not with dead bricks and mortar but with living bricks which together should grow into a new temple, cemented together with the mortar of the Holy Spirit, the Lord and giver of life. The first Tower of Babel was a humanist enterprise, nicely calculated and laudable in its way, but it was really no more than the archetype of secular Empire, for it was undertaken without reference to God. Hence it was overthrown, and the unity of language that had bound men together was destroyed. The first Pentecost was the reversal of this, for everyone understood the Apostles as if they had been speaking in their own language. This was the foundation of the unity in diversity on which the new Tower of Babel, the new and living Temple was to be built. For Christ

is the living stone, rejected by men but chosen by God and precious to him; set yourselves close to him so that you too, the holy priesthood that offers the spiritual sacrifices which Jesus Christ has made acceptable to God, may be living stones making a spiritual house. As scripture says: See how I lay in Zion a precious cornerstone that I have chosen and the man who rests his trust on it will not be disappointed.[42]

[41] Acts, I. 14.   [42] I Peter, 2. 4–6.

This is the promise made to the believers:

but for unbelievers, the stone rejected by the builders has proved to be the keystone, a stone to stumble over, a rock to bring men down. They stumble over it because they do not believe in the word; it was the fate in store for them.[43]

And whose fault was that? Not the unbelievers' surely, for they quite genuinely could not and cannot see in the Catholic Church a 'spiritual house' founded on the 'key-stone' of Jesus Christ and built up of 'living stones', for the living stones are for the most part sinful men, and the spiritual union experienced at Pentecost was simply the embryonic promise, not the adult fulfilment of what we have come to call the Communion of Saints. This cannot be stressed often enough: the Church has the guarantee but it has not yet the fulfilment. For the world is still in travail, and the Church, the body of the new Adam, is perhaps only now reaching puberty. Its struggles and its sins might be compared to the teething troubles and the infantile diseases that are the lot of all children. The Church, as the body of Christ, is a living organism, subject always and inexorably to the diseases which we call sin. If it is free of the measles, it has probably got the mumps; and if it is cured of whooping-cough, it will probably get chicken-pox. So is it with the Church and its collective sins. But the root-cause of sin is always the same: a collective egoism is put in the place of the free working of the Holy Spirit which, unlike Jesus Christ who after all is the founder of the Christian Church only, is the universal Spirit who gives life to all religions, whether Semitic, Indian, or Chinese. It is the Holy Spirit in Christianity re-appearing as the *rūḥu'l-qudus* in the Koran; it is the *prāna* of the Upanishads and the drive of evolution. But always and everywhere it is thwarted by man's efforts to find a collective *brāhmī sthitiḥ*, a 'fixed, still state of Brahman', in a world that is irremediably in flux.

No, we have not been redeemed, we have not been set

---

[43] Ibid., 2. 7–8.

free; we are still abnormal, and although in Jesus Christ as Logos our true 'normality' has been revealed to us, we cannot really accept it because our enemy, the Devil is still 'prowling round like a roaring lion, looking for someone to eat'[44]. So Peter: and now Paul.

It was not for any fault on the part of creation that it was made unable to attain its purpose, it was made so by God; but creation still retains the hope of being freed, like us, from its slavery to decay, to enjoy the same freedom and glory of the children of God. From the beginning till now the entire creation, as we know, has been groaning in one great act of giving birth; and not only creation, but all of us who possess the first-fruits of the Spirit, we too groan inwardly as we wait for our bodies to be set free. For we must be content to hope that we shall be saved—our salvation is not in sight, we should not have to be hoping for it if it were—but, as I say, we must hope to be saved since we are not saved yet—it is something we must wait for with patience.[45]

Teilhard too, optimist though he certainly was, saw that no evolution was possible without suffering and sin, that 'hell is the natural corollary of heaven,'[46], and that every success in one field must be paid for by failure in another. The crucifixion and resurrection have a cosmic dimension, and the suffering of the one and the glory of the other cannot be dissociated.

The more refined and complex mankind becomes, the more numerous do the chances of disorder become and the more does the gravity of them come to the fore; for you cannot raise up a mountain without digging an abyss; and every energy is equally powerful either for good or for evil. Everything that *becomes* suffers or sins. The truth about our position in this world is that *in it we are on the Cross.*

[But] . . . on Calvary [Christ] is still, and above all, the centre onto which all earthly sufferings *converge* and in which they *find peace.* We have very little evidence about the way our Lord experiences his mystical body in order to take delight in it, but we can get some idea of how he can gather to himself its sufferings;

---

[44] 1 Peter, 5. 8.   [45] Romans, 8. 20–25.
[46] *Écrits du temps de la guerre*, p. 58.

and the only way we can appreciate the immensity of his agony is to see in it an anguish which reflects all anguish, a *'cosmic'* *suffering*. During the Passion Christ felt the weight of all human sorrows bearing down upon his soul, alone and crushed—in an amazing synthesis no words can describe.[47]

The Passion is the necessary obverse of the Resurrection; and both must be reflected in the Body of Christ which is the Church and, beyond the Church, in all mankind as it is carried along irreversibly, as Teilhard would say, to its cosmic destiny in the cosmic Christ.

> As he is the Beginning,
> he was the first to be born from the dead,
> so that he should be first in every way;
> because God wanted all perfection
> to be found in him
> and all things to be reconciled through him and for him,
> everything in heaven and everything on earth,
> when he made peace
> by his death on the cross.[48]

Christ, because he is both God and man, is the Centre to which all human 'centres', all human 'selves' as 'parts of God', as the Gītā (15.7) puts it, must look. He is the mid-point in human evolution, midway between the 'beginning' when 'God's Spirit hovered over the water' and the final Parousia when 'God will be all in all'[49]. Father, Logos, and Holy Spirit—co-equal, no doubt, in eternity, with logical priority assigned to the Father; but, as manifested in time, first the Holy Spirit 'veiled' in matter and 'emptied' into it. Second, the Logos, 'veiled' and 'emptied' into the Man-God, Jesus, crucified and resurrected, present but still veiled both in his sacramental body which is the food of his mystical body, the Church, and in the mystical body itself which is or rather will be that divine 'association in which the free development of each will be the condition for the free development of all', the dream of Marx and Aurobindo.

---

[47] Ibid., p. 56: cf. E.T. *Writings in Time of War*, p. 67.
[48] Colossians 1. 18–20.   [49] 1 Corinthians, 15. 28.

But, as Teilhard warns, human freedom can only mean that we are at liberty to opt out of the evolutionary process which inevitably leads to the union and spiritualization of all that can be saved in Christ; for, if Scripture tells us anything, it is that only a remnant can be saved; and evolution too shows an enormous wastage in this our pilgrimage from the pure dissociation of matter to the final state of spiritualization and integration, the 'redeemed' body of Christ. This is the dark side of the picture, and it is not unknown to Hinduism; for in the Gītā there is not only a *paramā gatiḥ*, the 'highest way', which is timeless and eternal, there is also an *adhamā gatiḥ*, the 'lowest way', which presumably must be the same.

Birth after birth in this revolving round, these vilest among men, strangers to all good, obsessed by hate and cruel, I ever hurl into devilish wombs. Caught up in devilish wombs, birth after birth deluded, they never attain to me: *and so they tread the lowest way.*[50]

What then is lacking? It is not difficult to see: and St. John has told us with his usual devastating candour:

> We can be sure that we know God
> only by keeping his commandments.
> Anyone who says, 'I know him',
> and does not keep his commandments,
> is a liar,
> refusing to admit the truth.[51]

And, according to the same John, Jesus himself had said:

> I give you a new commandment:
> love one another;
> just as I have loved you,
> you also must love one another.[52]

We have not loved one another, and the world has therefore not known that we are his disciples. The world has said to us and still says to us what Jesus said to the religious establishment of his day:

Woe unto you, scribes and Pharisees, hypocrites! You who

[50] Bhagavad-Gītā, 16. 19–20.   [51] 1 John, 2. 3–4.   [52] John 13. 34.

travel over sea and land to make a single proselyte, and when you have him you make him twice as fit for hell as you are.[53]

Teilhard would have us believe that, evolutionarily speaking, the Christian Church is a phylum of love. So far the record is on the whole against him. Only the mystics have learnt to love God, the Centre of all centres, and most of them have not been able to correlate this with love of their neighbour. With the universalization of love which Teilhard, in a more typically optimistic mood, foresees, all men will have something of the mysticism of love which is, after all, the specifically Christian contribution to the mystical complex. And so he says:

As the mystics felt and foresaw, everything becomes physically and literally lovable in God; and, conversely, God can be grasped and loved in everything around us. In the breadth and depth of its cosmic matter, in the bewildering number of the elements and events of which it is made up and in the wide sweep too of the bountiful currents which dominate it and carry it forward like a single great river, the world, filled as it is with God, can only appear to our eyes once blind but now wide open as a *milieu* and an object of universal communion.[54]

What can this mean except that every action, once it is directed towards [Christ], assumes, without any change in itself, the psychic character of a centre to centre relationship, in other words, an act of love. . . .

And so organized matter, directed towards the Super-Christ, converges on itself. Just as countless tints combine in nature to produce a single white light, so do the infinite modes of action merge, without losing their identity, into a single colour under the powerful influence of the universal Christ; and in this movement it is love that marches in the van, love seen not simply as the common factor through which the multiplicity of human activities achieves its cohesion, but as the higher, universal, and synthetized form of spiritual energy in which all the other energies of the soul are transformed and sublimated, once they fall within 'the field of God-as-end (Omega).'[55]

[53] Matthew, 23. 15.
[54] *Oeuvres* 9, p. 213: E.T., *Science and Christ*, p. 168.
[55] Ibid., p. 215: E.T., pp. 170–1.

Such is the *paramā gatiḥ*, the 'highest way'; but over against it stands the *adhamā gatiḥ*, the 'lowest way', the 'triple gate of hell'.

According to Teilhard, those who tread this way are the ones who have refused love, who have resisted the radiance of what he calls Christ-Omega, whose egos nothing can break apart. And so, at the end of *The Phenomenon of Man*, he presents us with two alternatives.

We can entertain two almost contradictory suppositions about the physical and psychical state our planet will be in as it ripens and draws near to its fulfilment.

According to the first hypothesis which expresses the hopes to-wards which we ought in any case to turn our efforts as to an ideal, evil on earth at its final stage will be reduced to a minimum. Disease and hunger will be conquered by science and we will no longer need to fear them in any acute form. And, conquered by the sense of the earth . . ., hatred and internecine struggles will have disappeared in the ever-warmer radiance of God-as-end. Some sort of unanimity will reign over the entire mass of the noosphere. The final convergence will take place *in peace*. Such an outcome would of course conform most harmoniously with our theory.

But there is another possibility. Obeying a law from which nothing in the past has ever been exempt, evil may go on growing alongside good, and it too may attain its paroxysm at the end in some specifically new form.

There are no summits without abysses.

Enormous power will be liberated in mankind by the inner play of its cohesion; though it may be that this energy will still operate discordantly tomorrow, as it does today and did in the past. Are we to foresee a mechanizing synergy under brute force [the Stalinist way][56] or a synergy of sympathy [the way of the Holy Spirit][56]? Are we to foresee man seeking to fulfil himself collectively upon himself, or personally upon a greater than himself? Refusal or acceptance of God-as-end. A conflict may supervene. In that case the noosphere, in the course of and in virtue of the process that draws it together, will, when it has reached its point of unification, split into two zones each attracted to an opposite pole of adora-tion. Thought has never been united upon itself here below. Uni-

[56] Author's addition.

versal love would, then, in the last instance only vivify and liberate a fraction of the noosphere, and thereby bring it to its consummation—the part which decided to 'cross the threshold', to get outside itself into the Other. . . .

[This will mean] the death of the materially exhausted planet; the split of the noosphere, divided on the form to be given to its unity; and simultaneously . . . the liberation of that percentage of the universe which, across time, space, and evil will have succeeded in laboriously synthetizing itself to the very end.[57]

Evolution will no doubt draw us together, but this drawing together may only result in a 'civilization' of the ant-hill, each doing his allotted task because, when all his material wants are satisfied, this will be enough for 'the inert and uninteresting mass of those who believe in nothing'[58]; or, by a miracle (and a real miracle is needed) the Catholic Church, re-invigorated and transformed once again by the power of the Holy Spirit, will, purged at last of the miserable legalism that has cramped and stunted her so long, grow inwardly into a super-consciousness manifesting itself in spontaneous love and joy, so that not only will she become the true Marxian 'association in which the free development of each is the condition for the free development of all', but also, having realized the kingdom of heaven within herself she may succeed in embracing the whole of humanity within the finally realized city of God on earth. The Catholic Church *de jure* might then become the Catholic Church *de facto*, and, who knows, perhaps, before the demise of this planet, having perfected herself on earth, she may be able (with the help of science the potentialities of which we can now, after the conquest of the moon, only dimly visualize) to spread the gospel of *sac-cid-ānanda*, of Being, Superconsciousness, and spontaneous Joy, the Catholic gospel of unity in Trinity through the power of the Holy Spirit, throughout the entire universe. The possibilities are literally infinite: but unless and until we have really learnt to love

[57] *The Phenomenon of Man*, E.T. (slightly modified), pp. 288–9.
[58] *Oeuvres 5*, p. 101.

without a trace of egoism or *amour-propre* we had better stay just where we are, awaiting the destruction that our egoisms, both individual and collective, will have brought upon us.

But let us not end on so gloomy a note; for Teilhard also said in a more typical vein:

Like an enormous tide Being will have got the better of the unquiet swell of beings. In the heart of an ocean calmed and tranquil but in which every drop will be conscious of remaining itself, the extraordinary adventure of the world will have come to an end. The dream of every type of mysticism will have found its full, legitimate satisfaction. *Erit in omnibus omnia Deus*: 'God will be all in all.'[59]

[59] *Oeuvres* 5, p. 403: E.T., *The Future of Man*, p. 308.

IV

UNITY IN DIVERSITY
VEDĀNTIN AND CHRISTIAN

THE Communion of Saints. This concept has been embedded in the Christian creed for centuries. Perhaps in those early days of apostolic fervour this typically Christian idea was a reality, and it may be true that Christians really did love one another; but even so one has only to read the letters of St. Paul to realize how constantly even these early Christians were backsliding. Communion, it seems, there was, but it was not a communion of saints, for Paul's new converts, as often as not, were not changed overnight from sinners into saints. To put it crudely, the rite of baptism was not automatically followed by the descent of the Spirit: the carnal man did not automatically become the spiritual man. Egoism is far too subtle a thing to give way so easily to selflessness. Even in the earliest days of the Church the corroding work of anti-Christ—of egoism, that is, in all its forms—was busily at work. True, the ideal of the Church as the living body of Christ had been magnificently sketched out by St. Paul, and for a little time, perhaps, he may have seen this as a reality, as a living organism and not simply as a well-ordered organization. There may have been a felt cohesion among Christians which gave them a sense of interconnectedness that set them apart from the individualistic and pluralistic society of the pagan Roman Empire. There was, if you like, a communion of would-be saints—the promise but not the reality. But there *was* the promise—the ideal not just of a community of believers in the Muslim sense but the ideal of a society as tightly knit together as is a human body, the body of the Man-God Christ himself, dead and resurrected in the Church he had founded. This was the substance of the Catholic Church and of the Catholic idea—the idea of coherence and totality in one living organism that one day was to embrace the whole world. This idea has never been far from the mind of Catholic Christianity, and in the course of history it has proved its weakness as well as its strength; its strength so long as it was a persecuted minority, its weakness once it became the dominant majority. In what sense, then, was it a weakness, for did not the conversion of Constantine assure the dominance of the Catholic religion? Of course it did, but this very dominance was at variance with the whole teaching of Christ who had overthrown all the accepted standards of the world in that he had taught that the first shall be last and the last shall be first. Even before his birth his mother, Mary, had paid tribute to God whose 'foolishness is wiser than human wisdom and [whose] weakness is stronger than human strength'[1]. For what had Mary to boast about? Nothing but her own insignificance. Hence she thanked her God in these unforgettable words:

My soul proclaims the greatness of the Lord
and my spirit exults in God my saviour;
because he has looked upon his *lowly* handmaid. . . .
He has shown the power of his arm,
and he has routed the proud of heart.
He has pulled down princes from their thrones and exalted the
   lowly.
The hungry he has filled with good things, the rich sent empty
   away.[2]

The new spirit that was to have been normative for Christianity was apparent in the very beginning. In the celebrated scene of the temptation of Jesus in St. Matthew it becomes absolutely explicit: Christ, the Son of God, is confronted by one who is also described in the *Book of Job* (1.6) as a 'son of God', Satan.

Taking him to a very high mountain, the devil showed him all

---

[1] 1 Corinthians, 1. 25.   [2] Luke, 1. 46–53.

the kingdoms of the world and their splendour. 'I will give you all these' he said, 'if you fall at my feet and worship me'. Then Jesus replied, 'Be off, Satan! For scripture says:

> You must worship the Lord your God,
> and serve him alone.'[3]

Jesus did not fall for this temptation, for his kingdom was not of this world. Once an Emperor was converted, however, the Church all too soon bowed to Satan, accepting temporal power and spurning the role of servant. From persecuted she became persecutor, imposing her Catholic unity by force, thus usurping the role and power of the Holy Spirit whose freedom and saving action she now did her best to hamper in her passion for what she conceived to be Catholicity. The Saviour's words were forgotten:

> Happy are you when people abuse you and persecute you and speak all kinds of calumny against you on my account. Rejoice and be glad, for your reward will be great in heaven; this is how they persecuted the prophets before you.[4]

Gandhi once said: 'There is an ineffaceable blot that Hinduism carries with it, ... this miserable, wretched, enslaving spirit of "untouchableness". .... It is, to my mind, a curse that has come to us; and so long as that curse remains with us, so long I think we are bound to consider that every affliction in this sacred land is a proper punishment for the indelible crime that we are committing.'

Substitute the word 'persecution' for 'untouchableness', and the same must hold good for the Catholic Church. It has been the 'ineffaceable blot' and the 'curse' that Western Christianity has carried with it ever since Augustine of Hippo gave the full weight of his authority to the persecution of heretics—persecution, that is, in the name of Catholicity and unity, no matter at what cost to the real organic unity that St. Paul had called the body of Christ.

Unity—this in one form or another is the theme of all 'higher' religion, and it is also, manifestly now, the trend of

---

[3] Matthew, 4. 8–10.   [4] Ibid., 5. 11–12.

evolution itself. But evolution does not work in a straight line, for it meets with obstructions on every side, and the obstructions are largely of its own making. These are those forms of life that have become stabilized, ossified, one might say, and seem to have lost their ability to develop or change. In political terms these call themselves the forces of stability, of established law and order and so on: they are the lesser unities of the past which seek to obstruct the greater unities that are yet to come. But, leaving that aside for the moment, let us first see how the great religions of the world conceive of unity, for until we understand this we are unlikely to understand one another. I think that a great obstacle in the way to any mutual comprehension between Vedāntin spirituality and Catholic Christianity is that so many Neo-Vedāntins see Vedānta everywhere, and what is not reducible to Vedānta they dismiss as irrelevant and unreal. Take, for example, this passage from a recent book by Mr. P. J. Saher called *Eastern Wisdom and Western Thought* (pp. 242-3):

The distinguishing hallmark of Eastern wisdom is that there is no controversy whatsoever as to the goal. . . . [For] its only excuse for existence is that it offers the essential as against the merely accidental, the eternal in place of the ephemeral, the transcendental instead of the transient (p. 240). . . . For it the individual is all important in his capacity as an individual. It is the good for which everyone, *as an individual*, has to strive, for that is the main topic of Eastern wisdom and not the good of any bundle of human beings, such as society, nation, humanity, proletariat or the like (p. 243).

This passage is worth quoting, for it is typical not only of the Neo-Vedāntin point of view, but also, to a very large extent, of higher religion in general. The Vedānta (and I am now using the word in its literal sense, the 'end of the Veda', that is the Upanishads) is obsessed with unity, and the unity is that of the eternal and timeless ground of the human self: Ātman is Brahman, if you like, though this often tends to be a tautology. What Mr. Saher, however, is saying is that every human being not only becomes and develops in time (and that is to him purely peripheral) but also eternally *is*. Hence the goal of life can only be the 'Self-Realization' of the individual as Ātman, the conquest of physical death by passing into one's true being where, since this is beyond time, it must also necessarily be beyond death. The goal of life, then, can only be the extinction of life, the *requies aeterna*, the 'eternal rest', for which Catholics pray on behalf of the departed. But this is only one side of the picture, and it is a mistake to take the part for the whole. It is also to mistake the Indian contribution for the whole of Eastern wisdom and arbitrarily to exclude the Chinese.

In an earlier work I contrasted prophetic religion with mystical religion, and I think the contrast holds. You have only to compare the immense emphasis Christian (and particularly Protestant) theologians put on the 'historicity' of God—the God of history, and so on—and contrast this with the overriding insistence of the Vedāntins on Brahman as pure Being and therefore unaffected by and indifferent to what goes on in this world, to realize that between these two points of view there is a gulf fixed. But this is not the only distinction we can draw between the higher religions: there is another, and it is at least as important. On the one side there are religions which concentrate mainly on *individual* salvation or 'liberation', and on the other there are those which see salvation as being applicable mainly to the group, nation, Empire, or ultimately the whole human race. Both Hinduism and Buddhism seem to be overwhelmingly individualistic so far as 'salvation' is concerned, whereas Confucianism, Judaism, and Islam think primarily in terms of the community: man sees himself as an integral part of the community and his salvation is inseparable from that of the community as a whole. He does not 'fare like the horn of a rhinoceros alone'[5] as does the perfected Buddhist sage. Moreover, the community is under divine

[5] *Suttanipāta*, 35ff.

guidance and it looks forward to the day when all things
will be made perfect. The exception here is Confucianism,
for the Confucians were able to establish a hierarchical and
static society governed, in theory at least, by the Confucian
Tao for a period of some eight hundred years. They considered that they had discovered an ideal social order in which a
perfect human harmony had ideally been achieved—a
harmony that reflected the harmony of Nature, of heaven
and earth with which man, the midpoint between the two,
formed a triad. They did not, then, look forward to an age
of renewal and perfection; but since, as the Buddhists so
rightly say, there is nothing that arises that does not pass
away, or, in the words of Ecclesiastes, that most Buddhist
book of the Old Testament, 'all is vanity,' they disappeared
never, it would seem, to rise again. Must this be the fate of
every communal religion?

I am well aware that to the Vedāntin with his thirst for
the eternal the time-bound religions of Judaism and Islam—and, for that matter, Christianity too—must appear
in some ways superficial, even childish; for it is true that man,
in so far as he is spiritual at all, longs for what does not pass
away. Though potentially a *kshetrajña*, a 'knower of the field',
he is actually an *a-kshetrajña*—he only sees the surface of the
field: he does not know that a treasure lies beneath it. For as
the Upanishad says:

Just as [a group of people] who do not know the country
(*akshetrajña*) might wander about and pass over a hidden hoard
of gold time and again without finding it, so too do all these
creatures go on day after day without finding the Brahman-
world within them, for they are led astray by unreality.[6]

To find this treasure within is the overriding passion of
Hindu and Buddhist alike; for 'this is the Self, exempt from
evil, untouched by age or death or sorrow, untouched by
hunger or thirst, [the Self] whose desire is the real, whose
idea is the real.'[7]

---

[6] *Chāndogya* Upanishad, 8. 3. 2.   [7] Ibid., 8. 1. 5.

This is the 'hidden treasure' in all of us; and it is this that the Upanishads are constantly urging us to seek out. So too we find precisely the same simile in the Gospel according to St. Matthew:

> The kingdom of heaven is like treasure hidden in a field which someone has found; he hides it again, goes off happy, sells everything he owns and buys the field.[8]

The treasure which Jesus calls the 'kingdom of heaven' is also 'discernment' (*viveka*), the 'fear of the Lord' (meaning almost exactly what Hindus understand by *bhakti*), and the 'knowledge of God' (*jñāna*). For we read in Proverbs on which the passage from Matthew is based:

> If your plea is for clear perception,
>   if you cry out for *discernment*,
> if you look for it as if it were silver,
>   and search for it as for *buried treasure*,
> you will then understand what the fear of Yahweh is,
>   and discover the *knowledge* of God.[9]

This surely is the 'Self whose desire is the real, whose idea is the real'; and this is the 'kingdom of God within you'[10], the one thing worth having, the 'only goal' of religion as Mr. Saher would have us believe, the true abiding Self which is anchored in God. This is, of course, not the conscious ego which, in the last analysis, is the source of all our miseries as the Buddha so clearly saw, but our eternal essence, the *sac-cid-ānanda*, Being, Consciousness, and Joy, of the Hindus. And it is also the 'self' of which Jesus speaks: 'what gain,' he asks, 'is it for a man to have won the whole world and to have lost or ruined his very self?'[11]

And this is the lesson of the Gītā too, for there we read of those men 'who seek to build up wealth unjustly to satisfy their lusts,' men who apparently are strong, happy, and successful, 'puffed up with self-conceit, unbending, maddened by their pride in wealth, . . . hypocrites.' These too 'have

---

[8] Matthew, 13. 44. [9] Proverbs, 2. 3–5.
[10] Luke, 17. 21. [11] Luke, 9. 25.

won the whole world' but their destiny is 'the triple gate of hell, *destruction of the self.*'[12]

On this the two religions are agreed. To find your inmost self is to find freedom and immortality, for as the Muslim tradition also says: 'Who knows himself, knows his Lord'. But is this really the one goal of human life? Can the rejection of life as we know it really be the goal of *life*? And were the orthodox Christians so very wrong when they dubbed the Manichees who did precisely this as the *pessima haeresium*, as 'the worst of heretics'?

There are surely two sides to the picture of which this is only one; and to put this forward as an *integral* view of life, as Mr. Saher does, is to see only one side of the picture: it is to separate the eternal from the temporal, the infinite from the finite; and on the Christian side it is to deny all meaning to the Incarnation, the union of mortal man in all his degradation, his subjection to decay and death, his sheer fleshly and unspiritual nastiness, with the 'spiritual man' who is also God and who 'did not abhor the Virgin's womb', 'a cramped and filthy place', as a Zoroastrian text puts it.

The overwhelming tendency of Indian religion has been to avert one's gaze from the world and to seek for the abiding truth within:

A certain sage, in search of immortality,
Turned his eyes inward and saw the Self within.[13]

And what kind of Self did he find there?

When once one understands that in oneself
The Self has become all beings,
When once one has seen the unity,
What room is there for sorrow, what room for perplexity?[14]

This seems to be the central message of Hinduism—to find the unity of the whole cosmos reflected in oneself, for man is a microcosm made in the image of God as the

[12] Bhagavad-Gītā, 16. 12–17, 21.   [13] *Katha* Upanishad, 4. 1.
[14] *Iśā* Upanishad, 7.

Hebrew scripture says, but he is also made in the image of the world. For

> As wide as this space [around us], so wide is this space within the heart. In it both sky and earth are concentrated, both fire and wind, both sun and moon, lightning and the stars, what a man possesses here on earth and what he does not possess: everything is concentrated in this [tiny space within the heart].[15]

Or, in the words of Origen: 'Know that you are another world *in parvo* and that in you there is sun, and moon, and the stars as well.'[16]

This is the Self, the 'kingdom of God within you', the 'image and likeness of God' of which Genesis speaks. Its essence is unity, and in this unity there is abiding peace. But it is a unity that can only be experienced by an individual in himself. If anything, this experience of one's own inner and timeless unity separates you from your fellowmen, for you have realized that at the core of your being you are sufficient unto yourself. 'What room is there for sorrow, what room for perplexity?' What room indeed for anything other than this 'self'? For you have found the 'hidden treasure' in your heart.

Nobody knows how religion started and it would be foolish to speculate on this theme; but it seems clear that we can no longer speak of a single ancestor of the human race, no Adam, no Manu, no Gayōmart; for as the fourteenth-century English mystic, Julian of Norwich, saw: 'in the sight of God all man is one man [Adam], and one man is all man,'[17] and it is only when this All-man becomes differentiated and fully self-conscious as 'all men' that our troubles and hatreds and jealousies become possible. There never was a Garden of Eden, there never was a Fall, man never was an angel riding serenely upon his obedient 'brother ass', the body; he was simply a beast endowed not with self-consciousness but with what Teilhard de Chardin called

---

[15] *Chāndogya* Upanishad, 8. 1. 3.   [16] *Hom. in Leviticum*, 126. 5. 2.
[17] *Revelations of Divine Love*, chap. 51.

co-consciousness, a communal consciousness shared by the whole human race as it was rising inexorably towards a state of full self-consciousness when it learnt to say 'I'. Religion, it seems to me, is man's reaction to the human situation as it develops when Adam, the All-man, becomes 'all men', each separated from the other and feeling himself alone and afraid. The religious reaction to this can be either 'inward' or 'outward'. The problem is how to restore the shattered harmony. In India man 'turned his eyes inward and saw the self within'. In China the Taoists did much the same or rather they looked *back* to a vanished golden age when, since the individual had no consciousness apart from the group, he could live with the life of the group in a state of co-consciousness, feeling himself to be at one with all things, 'rocked like a child by the great Mother in whose arms he has just woken'[18]. This is to relapse into that innocence which is at the same time ignorance, as Rousseau said, and a refusal to grow up even after tasting the forbidden fruit of the tree of the knowledge of good and evil. But, as the *Brihadāranyaka* Upanishad (1.4.1) says, 'a man who is all alone is afraid,' or, in the words of Genesis (2.18), 'it is not good that the man should be alone.' And so newly self-conscious man seeks to re-establish a simulacrum of a lost co-consciousness in the social organization of his tribe and the religious rites that bind it together. This was the way of Confucius, the establishment of a new and higher, because fully self-conscious, harmony in which ritual was to restore the former un-selfconscious co-consciousness of the mass. This too was the way of Israel, and it seems to have worked at first in both cases: the lost sense of 'immortality' was found not 'within' but 'without', not in solitude but in religious solidarity with one's fellow-men. Thus, broadly, we may speak of the religions of solitude (India and Taoism) and the religions of solidarity (Israel, Confucianism, and later Islam).

[18] Teilhard, *Écrits du temps de la guerre*, p. 19: E.T., *Writings in Time of War*, p. 28.

We have shown that Christianity agrees with Hinduism in that it insists that the immortal self can only be found if the empirical self, the 'I', dies. This is the first thing necessary, for until the ego dies, the 'self' cannot emerge into that eternal life which is its birthright. Similarly, until he has been crucified with Christ, Paul cannot say, 'I live now not with my own life but with the life of Christ who lives in me.'[19] This is, of course, the aspect of Christ which the Neo-Vedāntins emphasize at the expense of all others—the indwelling God; but it is only one aspect as we shall see. And, of course, to live with the life of Christ does not mean simply to sink or rise into or rediscover a timeless joy within (although it means that too), but also to live as Christ lived and as Paul lived, selflessly in the service of other men. This is the meaning of the words:

> Unless a wheat grain falls on the ground and dies,
> it remains only a single grain;
> but if it dies,
> *it yields a rich harvest.*[20]

The death of the single grain is the Buddhist Nirvāna, to 'become Brahman' as the Gītā puts it, but, as in the Gītā, this is still not enough: the man who has become Brahman, who has been reborn in Christ, must then grow into ever fuller being, must 'yield a rich harvest'. For Christ is not only the still centre of our soul, the *brāhmī sthitiḥ*, the 'fixed, still state of Brahman', of which the Gītā (2.72) speaks; he is also 'the power and wisdom of God'[21], the *jñāna* and *śakti* of Śiva.

The kingdom of heaven is like a treasure hidden in a field which someone has found; he hides it again, goes off happy, sells everything he owns and buys the field.

The hidden treasure, as we saw, is discernment, the fear of the Lord, and knowledge of God: it is that power which enables us to distinguish the eternal from the perishable.

[19] Galatians, 2. 20. [20] John, 12. 24. [21] 1 Corinthians, 1. 24.

The 'field' is the *kshetra* of the *Chāndogya* Upanishad under which lies the 'hidden hoard of gold'—our material and animal form which we must first know and use if we are ever to extract the hoard of gold itself which is our own true and timeless self. The man who finds it, formerly *akshetrajña*, 'no knower of the field', must become a *kshetrajña*, a 'knower of the field': he must know both the field and the immortal treasure which it conceals. He therefore buys the field from the *kshetrin*, the 'owner of the field', who is God. But the treasure and the field go together, for the gold of immortality must not be separated from the fruitful field of evolutionary growth as is so often the case in Indian religion. Rather, the static, immutable 'self' must grow in and through the field of matter, time, and space so that it may 'have life and have it to the full'[22], life through which it may 'yield a rich harvest'. First, then, the kingdom of heaven within you must be sought out; but there is also the business of building the city of God on earth of which Aurobindo speaks. Well, there is another parable in the same chapter of St. Matthew which may be relevant:

> The kingdom of heaven is like a mustard seed which a man took and sowed in his field. It is the smallest of all the seeds, but when it has grown it is the biggest shrub of all and becomes a tree so that the birds of the air come and shelter in its branches.[23]

The seed that was sown is God's 'seed'[24], the Holy Spirit, by whom the man Jesus was conceived. But we must go back a little further to see what happened to the human race after 'all man' became 'all men'. The unity represented by Adam, the All-man, the Purusha of the *Purusha-sūkta*, whose unity was sacrificed on the altar of diversification and plurality— this unity was lost, and man himself was lost, not knowing how to utilize his newly found self-consciousness. Having once said *aham*, 'I', he put it into the genitive case and said *mama*, 'mine'. Egocentricity begat acquisitiveness, and between them they became the bane of mankind, for the

[22] John, 10. 10.   [23] Matthew, 13. 31–2.   [24] 1 John, 3. 9.

Buddhists the root-sin or rather the basic ignorance (there is really not very much difference since the Greek ἁμαρτία ('sin') means 'going astray' or 'getting things wrong'), but for the Catholics a *vere necessarium peccatum*, an 'absolutely necessary sin', since without it man could never have progressed; for there has first to be sin, that is, 'sundering' before there can be a uniting on a higher level. This re-uniting is precisely what the Confucians tried to achieve in China and for centuries they were astonishingly successful, for what they sought to do was to unite a whole people by concentrating it into a single point, the Emperor, the Son of Heaven, the 'Son of God'. This seems to have been the pattern throughout the civilized world: everywhere we find kings deified as the centre of their particular civilization, in Egypt and Mesopotamia, later in the Achaemenian Empire in Persia and the Mauryas and Guptas in India and, of course, the successive dynasties in China itself. Only on the Mediterranean littoral did this pattern fail to develop. Both Athens and Rome got rid of their kings at a very early date, keeping the name only as a religious function, while Israel, hitherto ruled by Yahweh himself (or so the Bible says), because she regarded kingship as a usurpation of the divine sovereignty, showed reluctance to establish a monarchy; and when she finally experimented with human kings, she did so to her lasting undoing.

Thus we see on the one hand a tendency in Asia for nations to group themselves into ever larger units around a king, but in the last resort these units owed their origin to aggressive force and by repressive force they were maintained until, each in its turn, they were overthrown by one stronger than themselves. On the Mediterranean littoral, for better or for worse, individualism, the conscious exploitation of individual self-consciousness, asserted itself in all its vigour until here too the petty Greek and other states were finally subjected to Rome which, once it had conquered the Mediterranean world, realized that it could no longer tolerate individual rivalries in its midst and, together with the conquered territories, submitted itself to Caesar. Always, however, and not only in the Mediterranean world there were two contrary forces at work against each other—an atavistic desire to unite on the one hand and a craving to retain individual liberty on the other. What men were looking for (however unconsciously) was the Marxian 'association in which the free development of each is the condition for the free development of all'. But such a development is scarcely possible except when the will of each coincides with the will of all, and the condition of this is that 'all men', that is, in the long run the whole human race once again become the 'All-man', but this time on a higher plane. But, as Julian of Norwich says, 'All man is one man and one man is all man'. Hence just as Adam, the 'one man', became all men, so must all men be compressed into the compass of one man, just as, on the scale of the microcosm, 'both sky and earth, both sun and moon, lightning and the stars are concentrated in this tiny space within the heart'.

As St. Paul says: 'Sin entered the world through one man, and through sin death, and thus death has spread through the whole human race because everyone has sinned.'[25] What, then, was this 'absolutely necessary sin of Adam' through which death entered the world? It was the All-man's 'Fall' from a state of innocence and ignorance into a state of individual consciousness, into what Genesis calls the knowledge of good and evil, a knowledge of the distinction between life and death. This sin was a 'sundering' of the individual from the totality: he not only dies but knows he has to die. In the state of co-consciousness the death of each was, so to speak, subsumed into the life of the All because each lived by the life of the All and therefore had no knowledge or fear of individual death. Sin, then, in this context must mean primarily the birth not only of the ego, now conscious of death, which, because it knows it must die, wishes to 'have life' here and now and to 'have it to the full'. Hence the ego gives birth to egoism which longs not only to be but also to

[25] Romans, 5. 12.

have and sets itself up in antagonism to other egos which must inevitably oppose his will and interests with theirs.

Adam was and is the All-man, the cosmic Man, the Purusha of the Rigvedic hymn: he had to die so that individual men might come to be. By 'sinning' he became a mutually antagonistic mass of individuals, tribes, and nations capable of uniting only against a common peril. True, Adam, and with him the whole human race, was made 'in the image and likeness of God', and since, as the Gītā says, all men are in their essence 'minute parts of God', it still remained open to them to refashion the image within themselves and 'see the self within', to see the changeless spirit inhabiting their mortal frame. This is the way that India discovered, but it discovered the deathlessness of Nirvāna at the price of making nonsense of saṁsāra—life as all of us with practically no exceptions have to live it here on earth. For we have no right to forget what the Gītā (7.3) itself says: 'Among thousands of men but one, maybe, will strive for self-perfection, and even among these athletes of the spirit who have won perfection's crown but one, maybe, will come to know me as I really am.' That is to say that only one in thousands can realize his own true self, the image of God within him. For the rest this can only be a matter of faith; for all religion is symbolic of a truth that cannot adequately be expressed. Faith makes you believe what you have not experienced: it is, in the strictest sense of the word, make-believe. If, then, individual 'liberation' is for the vast majority of mankind no more than make-believe, what are we to say of the collective salvation that both Christianity and Marxism offer? That too is make-believe, and we can only repeat what Uddālaka Āruni said to his son Śvetaketu who could not believe that a huge fig-tree could grow out of something he could not even see: 'Have faith.'[26] This is the same faith that St. Paul had—faith in that 'finest' and invisible 'essence' from which the huge tree of the Church was to grow up.

[26] *Chāndogya* Upanishad, 6. 12. 3.

This 'finest essence' was what Jesus had called a mustard seed, the 'nothing at all'[27] out of which 'the biggest shrub of all' was to grow.

'The kingdom of heaven is like a mustard seed which a man took and sowed in his field.' In order that divided mankind might find a living centre around which it might grow together, this 'finest essence', this Holy Spirit, which pervades all things as salt pervades the entire ocean[28], this same Holy Spirit which in the beginning 'hovered over the water'[29] and fertilized it, had to be concentrated in one place. The 'greater than the great' had to become 'the more minute than the minute'[30], the 'Golden Embryo'[31], who 'once born' was yet to be 'the Lord of every being . . . by whom strong heaven and earth are held in place'; for this more minute than the minute was also 'the image of the unseen God and the first-born of all creation'[32], 'the radiant light of God's glory and the perfect copy of his nature, sustaining the universe by his powerful command'[33], yet destined to 'empty himself and assume the condition of a slave and become as men are'[34]. This 'smallest of all seeds' had to be sown in a plot of land, an insignificant speck in the great *kshetra*, the great 'field', of matter, so that it might become the focus and centre of all ensouled matter which constitutes mankind. And so the spiritual 'seed' entered a Virgin's womb and a new All-man was born whose name was Jesus, 'God saves', and Emmanuel, 'God among us'.

'If it is certain,' St. Paul says, 'that through the fall of one man (the All-man Adam) so many died, it is even more certain that divine grace, coming through the one man, Jesus Christ, came to so many as an abundant free gift.'[35] Jesus Christ, modern theology insists, is a mystery, and so he is; and he needs to be interpreted in different ways to different generations and different cultures. The same is true of the doctrine

---

[27] Ibid., 6. 12. 1.　　[28] Ibid., 6. 13: *Brihadāranyaka* Upanishad, 2. 4. 12.
[29] Genesis, 1. 2.　[30] *Katha* Upanishad, 2. 20: *Śvetāśvatara* Upanishad, 3. 20.
[31] Rig-Veda, 10. 121.　　[32] Colossians, 1. 15.　　[33] Hebrews, 1. 3.
[34] Philippians, 2. 7.　　　　　　[35] Romans, 5. 15.

of the Holy Trinity which has been a stumbling-block to so many and which, though a fundamental dogma of the Christian Church and one to which Christians tenaciously adhere, has never been and probably never can be satisfactorily explained. What I tried to point out in the last chapter was that even if no rational explanation of the Trinity is possible, we are none the less at liberty to speculate on it in a way that might have meaning for ourselves. The Trinity, it seems to me, is more adequately reflected in Hinduism than in any other religion, but not in the artificial triad of Brahmā, Vishnu, and Śiva seen as the creator, preserver, and destroyer of the universe, for Brahmā has no significance in his own right, and Vishnu and Śiva are simply names and extrapolations of the supreme Deity seen as Person by their devotees. No, the true parallel is the Vedāntin Trinity *sac-cid-ānanda*, Being, Consciousness, and Joy. 'Being' is the Absolute, the absolutely transcendent, but also the 'Father, giver of the seed', as the Gītā (14.4) puts it, 'the seer, the Father', who 'sat on the high-priest's throne'[36], 'he who is the overseer in highest heaven'[37], God transcendent, the 'Person than whom there is nothing higher, the goal and the all-highest Way'[38]. The second aspect or 'Person' in its original meaning of 'mask' or 'character' is *cit*, 'consciousness' or 'thought', the Logos or rational principle through which all things cohere and are what they are in the context of an all-embracing unity. This is the principle of which it is written:

> In him were created
> all things in heaven and on earth:
> everything visible and everything invisible,
> Thrones, Dominations, Sovereignties, Powers—
> all things were created through him and for him.
> Before anything was created, he existed,
> and he holds all things in unity.[39]

[36] Rig-Veda, 10. 81. 1.   [37] Ibid., 10. 129. 7.
[38] *Katha* Upanishad, 3. 11.   [39] Colossians, 1. 16–17.

This is the *cit-śakti* of Aurobindo, the rational principle and as it were the blueprint of the universe, the 'self which consists of consciousness'[40], the 'Supermind' and the Logos. But this Logos in whom and by whom and for whom all things were created is also the eternal life by which Paul lived and which he identified with Christ, the 'more minute than the minute' which is yet 'greater than the great' who is 'hidden in the heart'[41] of men.

Last there is the Holy Spirit, the God who is Love[42], the 'seed'[43] from which the new Adam, the spiritual All-man was born, substantial 'peace and joy'[44]—the *ānanda* of the Hindu Trinity. What place, then, does the Holy Spirit occupy in the total Godhead? Primarily he is the love that unites the Father to the Son, Being to the Logos. But this love is also creative, the equivalent of sexuality in the eternal world. In Hinduism the Holy Spirit would correspond to the love that unites Śiva to his Śakti, that Power in whom 'were created all things in heaven and earth'. In the words of the *Śiva-jñāna-siddhiyār* (3.2.77): 'Śiva begets Śakti and Śakti begets Śiva. Both in their happy union produce the worlds and souls. Still Śiva is [ever] chaste and the sweet-speeched Śakti remains [ever] a virgin. Only sages can comprehend this secret.' This is very true of the Christian Trinity too.

There is, however, a difference between the Śakti of the *Śaiva Siddhānta* and the Christian Logos: the one is female and the other is male. This can be explained by the fact that Śakti is not only creatrix but also creation, matter, while the Logos is rather the blueprint and exemplar of the created universe. Moreover, the Logos is also the Son of the Father whereas Śakti is Śiva's eternal consort—a very much more natural concept. How, then, does God 'beget' or 'generate' his eternal Son 'through whom all things were made' except through something akin to a female principle? Perhaps the answer can be found in Genesis where we read (1.27):

---

[40] *Kaushītkī* Upanishad, 3. 9.
[41] *Katha* Upanishad, 2. 20: *Śvetāśvatara* Upanishad, 3. 20.
[42] I John, 4. 8.   [43] Ibid., 3. 9.   [44] Romans, 14. 17.

> God created man in the image of himself,
> in the image of God he created him,
> *male and female he created them.*

This implies that the Hebrew God was originally thought of as containing both the male and female principles in himself: like Śiva he reconciled this most fundamental pair of opposites. Reconciliation is love, and love is *ānanda*, 'joy', the joy that is experienced in sexual union. This 'joy-in-love' is the Holy Spirit who, like Śiva, is both *alinga*,[45] 'beyond sexuality and beyond distinguishing mark', and *linga*, the generative power that infuses life into matter and the joy inherent in this as in all creative acts. Thus alone among the so-called 'Persons' of the Holy Trinity the Holy Spirit is sexually ambivalent, for Spirit is beyond sex and gender; and indeed in Hebrew (and Arabic) it is feminine (*ruach, rūḥ*), in Latin masculine (*spiritus*), while in Greek it is neuter (πνεῦμα). So too we read in the Upanishad: 'It is not male, not female, nor yet hermaphrodite.'[46] And yet it is the spiritual 'seed' by which a man is regenerated and born anew, for, as St. John again says:

> No one who has been begotten by God sins;
> because God's seed remains inside him,
> he cannot sin when he has been begotten by God.[47]

This 'seed' can only be the Holy Spirit, for 'what is born of the flesh is flesh; what is born of the Spirit is spirit.'[48] So too the Spirit that 'hovers over the waters' of chaos fructifies them: in Hindu terms this is the entrance of Purusha into Prakriti—the spiritual fructification of matter. In this way it is the third 'Person' of the Holy Trinity who is the first to appear in time: he appears as the *creator Spiritus*, but in so doing he 'empties' himself of his godhead, assuming, not as in the case of the second Person, the Logos, the 'condition of a slave', but the condition of inert matter which, now ensouled by him, struggles forward towards life and conscious-

---

[45] *Śvetāśvatara* Upanishad, 6. 9.   [46] Ibid., 5. 10.
[47] 1 John, 3. 9.   [48] John, 3. 6.

ness. Here the 'seed' of God enters into the 'womb' of chaotic matter to give birth to Adam, the All-man, born from 'the dust from the soil' but ensouled by the Spirit of God. Matter, then, is the negative aspect of the Hindu Śakti, the female principle called into existence by a Trinity which, while containing within itself the 'blueprint' of femininity, is in its relationship to the created order, male, as it is to the soul of the mystic which plays the female to the divine Male, and to the Church, the bride of Christ. Begotten by the Holy Spirit and born of matter, the All-man then becomes 'all men'. His unity is broken, and a new spiritual centre for the human race had therefore to be found. The seed of God entered into the womb of Mary and 'the Word was made flesh'. Mary, then, was the 'field', the *kshetra*, and the 'furrow', *Sītā*, from out of whom the 'biggest shrub of all' would grow—'a tree in whose branches the birds of the air will come and shelter'.

Christ, the new Adam, then, was the focus around which a new, regenerated humanity was to take shape: he is the 'head' of his own body which was to be the Church.[49] According to Christian belief he is man but at the same time God: in Hindu terminology he is like all other men, 'being as all men are,' an eternal and timeless being in a specific psycho-somatic organism. His death on the Cross would then symbolize the death of the whole psycho-somatic being which is, strictly speaking, the 'not-self', and his resurrection would symbolize the emergence of the pure Ātman from its mortal shell. But this is not what the Christian understands by the crucifixion and resurrection because Christianity, like Judaism from which it emerged, is primarily a communal religion, individual salvation being only subsidiary to the salvation and deification of the whole human race. Moreover, it is not only the *ahaṁkāra* (the ego) that has to die, but the Ātman too, for there is a selfishness of the Ātman as much as there is a selfishness of the ego. The Ātman can die in the sense that it can be 'lost' to the

[49] Colossians, I. 18.

highest faculty in matter-born man, the *buddhi* or contemplative intellect with which it has a natural affinity, for, as the Gītā says, once *buddhi* is destroyed the whole man is destroyed, and this means the 'loss' or 'destruction' of the Ātman itself.[50]

Indian religion, whether Hindu or Buddhist is overwhelmingly concerned with *moksha*, the 'release' of the eternal and divine element in man from the purely material and temporal; it is concerned with the recovery of the 'image of God' and its separation from the 'dust from the soil' out of which in the process of millions of years self-conscious man had emerged. This the Mahāyāna Buddhists realized. And so we read in the *Lotus Sūtra* that the celestial Buddha, when he was about to deliver a totally *new* message to his self-perfected Arhats, had to chide them precisely for their 'transcendent' selfishness: 'before he can open his mouth to speak, five thousand of his disciples rise from their seats, salute him, and withdraw. "The root of sin was deep in them, and their haughty spirit was so enlarged that they imagined that they had already attained." The Buddha remains silent and does not stop them. "Now in this congregation," he says at last, "I am free from twigs and leaves, and have none but the true and real." '[51]

The 'root of sin' is also the root of ignorance: it is the root-sin and the root-ignorance shared, in this Mahāyāna view, by both the Sānkhya and the non-dualist Vedānta, the belief that once a man has realized his own timeless essence, once he has 'become Brahman' and entered Nirvāna, he has thereby reached a point beyond which it is impossible to proceed. In Hindu terminology, then, the Crucifixion would represent the death of the Ātman, the death of the deathless itself, the ultimate humiliation of spiritual pride dragged down to the 'triple gate of hell, destruction of the self'. This is what St. Paul tells us too in those amazing words addressed to the Philippians (2.6–8):

[50] Bhagavad-Gītā, 2. 63: 16. 21.
[51] See *The Lotus of the Wonderful Law*, ed. W. E. Soothill, Oxford, Clarendon Press, 1930, p. 68.

> His state was divine,
> yet he did not cling
> to his equality with God
> but emptied himself
> to assume the condition of a slave,
> and became as men are;
> and being as all men are,
> he was humbler yet,
> even to accepting death,
> death on a cross.

The *sadāmukta*, the man who is always free from the fetters of time, space and matter, has not only to enter into matter, confine himself in the cramped space of the womb of Mary, his *mater* and *materia*—his mother and 'matter'—but also to endure the ultimate indignity of suffering a felon's death on a wooden cross: 'cursed be everyone who is hanged on a tree.'[52] The 'tree' is also the 'wood' of creation of which the Rig-Veda speaks:

> What was the wood? What was the tree
> From which heaven and earth were fashioned forth?[53]

God, Viśvakarman, the 'Maker of all', fashioned forth the whole universe out of a primal 'wood', a primal ὕλη or matter. He becomes man, plies the trade of a carpenter— a fashioner of wood—and has then as Purusha, as the incarnate All-man, to be sacrificed on the same wood, the same matter he had created. Spirit is sacrificed on the wooden Cross, on matter in its most rudimentary form, in order that matter itself may once again be spiritualized.

The first thing the crucified Christ did, we are told in the Apostles' Creed, was to descend into 'hell', or as St. Peter puts it, 'he went to preach to the spirits in prison'[54]. Now what was this 'prison' to which these 'spirits' were confined? According to traditional Catholic teaching it was the Limbo of the Patriarchs, a place in which there is neither pleasure nor pain, a condition in which the opposites are transcended, a Nirvāna on the attainment of which those proud Arhats

---

[52] Galatians, 3. 13.   [53] Rig-Veda, 10. 81. 4.   [54] 1 Peter, 3. 19.

in the *Lotus Sūtra* thought there was no further to go. Here a man 'wins a prize beyond all others—*or so he thinks*',[55] as the Gītā tells us. 'Therein he [firmly] stands, unmoved by any suffering, however grievous it may be.'

We all know about the 'prison' of matter; but what the Cross and the 'descent into hell' teach us is that there is a prison of the spirit too, the prison of absolute *kaivalyam*, of absolute 'isolation', what the Sūfīs call *tafrīd*, the passionless Limbo of the Patriarchs. To be truly alive and eternally alive, then, man must die a second death and be born again in matter of some kind, what I suspect the Hindus mean by a 'subtle body', of which the resurrected body of Christ is the prototype. Ātman must be re-united with *buddhi*[56] so that it can again become conscious—realize itself as the *cit* as well as the *sat* in the Trinity of *sac-cid-ānanda*. To realize oneself simply as *sat* is 'to waste away in the spirit to which one restricts oneself' and 'to die of inanition'[57]. This is what personified matter tells man in Teilhard's little master-piece, *The Spiritual Power of Matter*. Perhaps it is not too far-fetched to put the same words into the mouth of the earthly Mary addressing her heavenly Son and warning him of how his future disciples will try to water down the full mystery of God made man and Spirit made matter:

You thought that you could do without her because the power of thought has been kindled in you! You thought that the more carefully you rejected what can be touched, the closer you would be to Spirit; that you would be more divine, if you lived in the world of pure ideas, or at least more angelic if you fled the body.

Yes, and you very nearly starved.

You need oil for your limbs, blood for your veins, water for your soul, the [concrete and] real for your mind;—you need all these because this is the very law of your nature. Do you understand? . . .

---

[55] Bhagavad-Gītā, 6. 22.
[56] See R. C. Zaehner in *Eranos-Jahrbuch*, 1963, Rhein-Verlag, Zürich, 1964, p. 304.
[57] Teilhard, *Écrits du temps de la guerre*, p. 439: E.T., *Hymn of the Universe*, p. 61.

Never say, as some say: 'Matter is worn out, matter is evil,' . . . for one has come who has said, . . . 'Life shall arise out of death,' and again uttering the final promise of my liberation, 'This is my body'.[58]

If Christ's 'descent into hell' means anything, it means that it restores to the dead their personalities now purified of all egoism and endowed with a 'super-consciousness' which draws them out of their 'isolation' in order that they may commune with their God and through him with one another. This too is what the Gītā (12.3–4) means when it says:

Those who revere the indeterminate Imperishable Unmanifest, unthinkable though coursing everywhere, sublime, aloof, unmoving, firm, who hold in check the complex of the senses, in all things equal-minded, taking pleasure in the weal of all contingent beings, these too attain to me.

By his resurrection Christ sanctifies our flesh and promises that we too will be resurrected in what St. Paul calls a 'spiritual body' or, as the Hindus would say, in a 'subtle body'. However we wish to explain this, it means that we will not be just identical spiritual monads as in the Sānkhya system but spiritual monads always capable of further growth and development as in Leibniz, enriched by their earthly experience and capable of loving God with a burning love and through God of loving and interpenetrating each other.

After the Resurrection, however, Christ ceases to be simply a man. He is the new All-man who is present all over the earth in the sacrament of bread and wine and in the living organism of the Church. Sacrament and Church represent the Catholic unity of the body of Christ; and since it is a 'body', this unity must be a unity in diversity just as is the Holy Trinity itself. In the Church the second 'Person' of the Trinity, the God who is both immanent and transcendent, grows throughout the ages of evolutionary time into the fully transcendent God so that when the two meet God may be 'all in all'[59].

---

[58] Ibid., pp. 440–1: E.T., pp. 63–4.   [59] 1 Corinthians, 15. 28.

Evolution, we can say, is the alienation of God from himself, his 'emptying' of himself into matter. The 'beginning' is the descent of the Holy Spirit into matter, welding it together in love and joy. And here again the Upanishad says: 'Who could breathe, who could live, were this joy not [diffused] throughout space?'[60] The Spirit enters matter, develops it into life and consciousness, and the first All-man, Adam, is born. The first Man, however, splits into a variety of mutually hostile individuals whose fundamental inability to co-operate is symbolized by the myth of Cain and Abel— an evil beginning if ever there was one to the humanist's idea of the brotherhood of man. The ideal of the collective personality of the religious community, however, was kept alive in Israel and China, and re-emerged in the West with the establishment of the Roman Empire; and it was precisely at this time of the triumph of the secular imperial idea that Jesus of Nazareth was born and brought the good news of the kingdom of heaven which was to take root on earth. Like the Purusha of the Vedic myth he dies a sacrificial death, but his body lived on both as sacrament—the spiritual and material food of his community—and as the community itself.

For centuries India had known as a matter of experience that the inmost core of the human being is immortal, not subject to death because, having its being outside time, it could not be affected by anything that takes place in time. Christ's sacrificial death on the Cross, however, does not simply mean the death of the ego as the essential condition for the emergence of the eternal self in all its timeless radiance: it also means that time and eternity, matter and spirit, Mary and the Holy Spirit who is the 'seed' of the Father, are joined and welded together in an inseparable union.

This union of spirit and matter is achieved both in the sacrament and the Church; and the breath by which the Church lives is that same Holy Spirit which 'in the beginning' hovered over the water, which infused life into Adam,

[60] *Taittirīya* Upanishad, 2. 7.

which entered the Virgin's womb as a spiritual 'seed', and which finally descended on the Apostles with Mary in their midst to restore the unity of the human race by abolishing, if only for a moment, the diversity of tongues which had separated man from man ever since men began to speak different tongues,—that second 'fall' symbolized by the myth of the Tower of Babel.

But—and it is an enormous 'but'—if—and it is an enormous 'if'—if the Church is indeed the 'mystical' body of Christ, living by the breath of the Holy Spirit, how are we to account for its disgraceful, blood-stained history? We have already suggested that the root-sin of the Church has, ever since the conversion of Constantine, been its betrayal of its spiritual mission in the interests of worldly power, and its total loss of Christ's gift of love which was made manifest in its mad and criminal career of persecution and intolerance. But in our dismay and horror at how the body of Christ has been recrucified by its own members in the course of its history, we should nonetheless remember that Christ, the Prince of peace, had also said with prophetic insight, 'It is not peace that I have come to bring, but a sword.'[61] Nor should we forget that we live in periods of time that are to be reckoned in millions rather than in hundreds of years in which 'a thousand years are a single day'[62], or, in the words of the Gītā (8.17): 'For a thousand ages lasts one day of Brahmā, and for a thousand ages one such night.' At the most then, the body of Christ can only now be reaching the age of puberty, a time of convulsion for the whole human race through which we are living now.

The Christian Church even now represents only a fraction of mankind, but ideally the body of Christ should encompass the whole human race—how and in what form—we have not the slightest idea. Like the human race, however, the Church sees itself as an organic unity in manifold diversity, in which the whole is tormented by the wickedness of the parts just as it is ennobled by the sanctity of the few. As St.

[61] Matthew, 10. 34.   [62] Psalm, 90. 4.

Paul says: 'Just as a human body, though it is made up of many parts, is a single unit because all these parts, though many, make up one body, so it is with Christ. . . . If all the parts were the same, how could it be a body? As it is, the parts are many, but the body is one. . . . [And so] if one part is hurt, all parts are hurt with it. . . . Now you together are Christ's body; but each of you is a different part of it.'[63] The parts are inseparable from the whole and live in and for the whole; and the bond of union between them is love: for, as St. Paul goes on to say, 'There are three things that last: faith, hope, and love; but the greatest of these is love.' Some of us have faith, fewer have hope, practically none of us has love; and without love there can be no Christianity. What we have advertised as Christianity has rarely been more than a caricature—make-believe, which makes fewer and fewer believe. Very few of us feel as a living reality that unity in diversity suffused by love that not only Christianity proclaims but also the Śaiva Siddhānta and the Vedānta according to Rāmānuja which have grown up independently on Indian soil. Must we then despair, and are not the world-denying ascetics after all right, secure as they are in their immunity from death and suffering because they know that in them dwells a 'Self exempt from evil, untouched by age or death or sorrow, untouched by hunger or thirst'[64]. Many Hindus themselves have begun to doubt this as the examples of Gandhi and Tagore, Sri Aurobindo, Radhakrishnan, and Vinoba Bhave, each in their personal and individual way, bear witness. Well, if Christians have wretchedly failed in their apostolate of love, let us not forget that they still have hope, *la petite espérance*, 'poor little hope,' as Charles Péguy puts it, and that traditionally despair is the sin against the Holy Spirit for which there is no forgiveness. It may be millions of years before the corporate ideal of the Church as the body of Christ even begins to look like reality, but the Holy Spirit has all eternity in which to work. So let us conclude with these realistic words of St. Paul:

[63] 1 Corinthians, 12. 12–27.   [64] *Chāndogya* Upanishad, 8. 7. 1.

The whole creation is eagerly waiting for God to reveal his sons. It was not for any fault on the part of creation that it was made unable to attain its purpose, it was made so by God; but creation still retains the hope of being freed, like us, from its slavery to decay, to enjoy the same freedom and glory as the children of God. From the beginning till now the entire creation, as we know, has been groaning in one great act of giving birth; and not only creation, but all of us who possess the first-fruits of the Spirit, we too groan inwardly as we wait for our bodies to be set free. For we must be content to hope that we shall be saved—our salvation is not in sight, we should not have to be hoping for it if it were—but, as I say, we must hope to be saved since we are not saved yet—it is something we must wait for with patience.[65]

[65] Romans, 8. 19–25.

APPENDIX

Address delivered on Founder's Day 1969 at
St. Stephen's College, Delhi

Today we have been giving thanks to God for all those who taught in this College and are now dead. Your Principal has asked me to address you during this Commemoration Service: appropriately enough, as it seems to me, since the full name of my own College in Oxford is the College of all the Souls of the Faithful Departed.

Before I left England St. Stephen's College was no more than a name to me. I have now been here for a week, and I can say with all the warmth of which my Anglo-Swiss heart is capable that I would not have thought it possible that in so short a time I could have grown to feel so completely at home anywhere. In England it never seems to occur to me that I am in a Christian country. In St. Stephen's I feel that the Holy Spirit of God is really, actually present. Particularly do I feel that it has blessed your Principal and his wife; through whose grace, unfailing kindness and unobtrusive attentiveness I have already come to love India and what Christians in India stand for. This has been for me a *Christian* experience; one which I cannot easily forget and for which I am deeply grateful. On this point there is nothing more for me to say except thank you and thank you again; *Shukriya, dhanyavad aur phir dhanyavad.*

Today I am speaking at a Commemoration service, speaking in honour of those amongst you who have left this world; not only of 'them who have left a name, so that men declare their praise', but also, and even more, of those 'who have left no memorial, who have perished as though they had not lived'. For in any Commemoration service we cannot but feel united in contemplating the one certainty that faces us all—the stark fact that we must all of us die. As a student of Comparative Religion I would say a few words on how other faiths than Christianity have thought of death. Since religion is largely concerned with man's attitude towards death this seems appropriate.

I think it is true to say that until comparatively modern times man has never quite accepted death as final; and it is, I think, largely the materialist acceptance of physical death as being total and final that is responsible for our present existentialist *malaise*. For if death is the snuffing out of the individual and the final end of all his aspirations, then life becomes an absurdity, and the only choices that are left to us are either suicide or having a good time while we can. Consciousness of the inevitability of death is perhaps the beginning of religion. It is what distinguishes man from the rest of the animal creation.

According to the Jewish myth Man (Adam) was created immortal and death entered the world through sin. Myths like this are common throughout the world. Today, when we are all conditioned by the theory of evolution, they seem singularly naive. I wonder whether they are necessarily so. Let us consider the Taoist myth which corresponds to the Golden Age of the Garden of Eden.

The True Man of ancient times knew nothing of loving life, knew nothing of hating death. He emerged without delight; he went back in without a fuss. He came briskly, he went briskly, and that was all. He didn't forget where he began; he didn't try to find out where he would end. He received something and took pleasure in it; he forgot about it and handed it back again.[1]

In other words he accepted things as they are. He lived not with his own life but with the life of the group. He had no sense of individuality and his individual death could therefore have no meaning for him, for the life of the group was immortal; his consciousness was a kind of common consciousness in and with the group, and since the group seemingly went on for ever, then individual death could be of no importance. But a time came when he ate of the tree of the knowledge of good and evil. He became conscious of himself as an individual. He learnt to say 'I'. As the Upanishad puts it:

In the beginning this universe was the Self alone—in the likeness of a man. Looking around he saw nothing other than himself. First of all he said: 'This is 'I'. . . . He was afraid. So even now a man who is all alone is afraid.[2]

And when we die we are alone; and unless we are supported by

[1] The Complete Works of Chuang Tzu, tr. Burton Watson, Columbia University Press, 1968, p. 78.

[2] *Brihadāranyaka* Upanishad, 1. 4. 1–2.

religious faith we are afraid. It is one of the functions of religion to enable us to conquer this fear.

'Till you know about the living, how are you to know about the dead?' Confucius had asked.[3] But Confucius was a sage, and most of us are not sages. We are worried about death and what it can mean.

Materialists will tell us that man's views concerning an afterlife are merely wishful thinking—an attempt to find compensation for the miseries of this world in a beatific hereafter. Are they?

The Jewish Sheol is scarcely a compensation for anything, nor is the Mesopotamian afterlife on which it is based. Think of this description of the afterlife from the *Epic of Gilgamesh*.

> I stood alone before an awful being; his face was sombre like the black bird of the storm. He fell upon me with the talons of an eagle and held me fast, pinioned with his claw, till I smothered; then he transformed me so that my arms became wings covered with feathers. He turned his stare towards me, and he led me away to the palace of Irkalla, the Queen of Darkness, to the house from which none who enters ever returns, down the road from which there is no coming back. There is the house whose people sit in darkness; dust is their food and clay their meat. They are clothed like birds with wings for covering, they see no light, they sit in darkness.[7]

This, surely, is scarcely wishful thinking. There is no compensation here. Simple annihilation would be far preferable to *this*. To be annihilated or to live for ever, which is the more dreadful prospect?

In a Christian context this may seem a paradoxical question, for did not Christ promise us eternal life? Certainly, but what kind of life? Too often we think of the joys of Paradise as being simply a continuation of our present life from which all suffering will have been eliminated—the life of the Hindu Devas, still lived in time and space in conditions not unlike what we are used to here on earth. This is not the way the Hindus think, and it seems to me that they are right.

It is true that their view of salvation is largely conditioned by their belief in re-incarnation. Life as lived on earth is repeated ever again, and the prospect of a literally endless series of more or less miserable lives is unbearable unless a way can be found which

---

[3] *Analects*, 11. 11.
[4] *The Epic of Gilgamesh*, tr. N. K. Sandars, Penguin Classics, 1960, p. 89.

will break the chain and deliver us for ever from conditioned human life as we know it. To the Hindu and the Buddhist 'eternal life' must seem more like hell than paradise; for life is, in St. Paul's words, enslavement to the body of this death; for to live is to suffer, as the Buddha saw, and salvation is Nirvāna, the putting to an end of suffering and pain. True, in Hinduism and Buddhism just as much as in Christianity it is assumed that good deeds are rewarded and evil deeds punished, and since Hindus and Buddhists believe in re-incarnation they are never faced with the predicament of Job. Good deeds will lead to a better incarnation, no doubt, but this is not enough; for we are still bound to the cycle of rebirth. Only a complete break with this endless flux of meaningless existence can bring rest to the soul; and *dona eis requiem aeternam* is quite as much a Hindu and Buddhist prayer as it is a Christian one: there can be no salvation in the world, and 'eternal rest' is death final and complete. *Dona eis requiem* is simply another way of saying *dona eis mortem*.

Does this seem strange to Christians? It should not, for we are told that Baptism is death. 'You have been taught that when we were baptised in Christ Jesus we were baptised in his death . . . and joined him in death.'[5] Obviously it must be so, for without death there can be no resurrection. It is very possible that in the early Church the new converts did really die to the old Adam and put on the second Adam; that is, they put away the ego which makes our individual lives the centre of our universe and by its selfishness is the root cause of all our miseries, and put on the risen Christ, the eternal Christ, who is conditioned by neither space nor time and is supremely free. This is no longer true; for how many of us can truthfully say that baptism meant any such thing to us? We all know that despite baptism we have not died to our carnal self, and that baptism can therefore be little more than a symbol of something that can only be consummated in our second baptism, our physical death, which alone can really set us free from the slavery of corruption and decay. But for Christians this second baptism, like the first, is not the end but a new beginning— and here there is a marked difference of emphasis between Christianity and the religions of Indian origin. For the Buddhist, *Nirvāna* is the end; and so too for the Hindus 'liberation' is the end. The Gītā, however, is the exception, and here it comes very near

[5] Romans, 6. 3–4.

to Christianity. For the 'Nirvana that is Brahma too', as the Gītā puts it, is not the end; it is only the beginning of life lived on another plane, the quality of which we know nothing about except insofar as the mystics have given us hints about it. The key-text in Christianity is John 12. 24—

> I tell you, most solemnly,
> unless a wheat grain falls on the ground and dies,
> it remains only a single grain;
> but if it dies,
> it yields a rich harvest.

This is, after all, at the heart of the Christian message, and it does, also, make sense in an Indian context. In order that your true self as it exists for all eternity in the sight of God may be born, the false self, the 'ego', must die; for it is the ego which sets itself up as an independent person, a centre that would exist independently of God and in competition and rivalry with all the other egos that surround it and with which it must live. Until that is dead there can be no awakening to that eternal life the nature of which we can descry only 'in a glass darkly', but which the mystics of all religions try to describe. After all, St. Paul has said it all before and what need have I to bother you with further discourse? 'When this perishable nature', he says, 'has put on imperishability, and when this mortal nature has put on immortality, then the words of scripture will come true: Death is swallowed up in victory. Death, where is your victory? Death, where is your sting?'[6]

For the same reason the Zoroastrians were forbidden to mourn their dead and quite rightly so, for as the Muslim Persian poet Jalālu'd-dīn Rūmī sings:

> On the day I die
> And my coffin moves out,
> Do not think, do not think
> That my heart is in this world.

> Do not weep for me and say,
> 'Woe is me, ah, woe is me!'
> For you would fall into Satan's trap
> And that would be woe indeed.

---

[6] I Corinthians, 15. 54–5.

When you see my hearse, do not say,
'Departed, passed away.'
For this is the time of meeting
And union of him with me.

When you hand me on to the grave
Do not say, 'Farewell, farewell.'
For the grave is the curtain concealing
The communion of paradise.

You have seen the downward passing;
Now look at the rising up.
Both sun and moon must set;
How should they suffer harm thereby?

To you it seems a setting;
In truth it is a rising.
The tomb seems like a prison;
It is the freeing of the soul.

What seed went down in the earth
That has not grown again?
Why then are you all doubtful
When it comes to the seed of man?

What bucket went down into the well
That did not come up full?
Why then should the soul which is Joseph
Complain about the well?

Though your lips are closed to this world
They will open in another;
For your song of jubilation
Is in a spaceless atmosphere.[7]

A spaceless atmosphere yes, and a timeless one too—the natural milieu in which our real souls dwell, as the Hindus never cease telling us. 'This is the self, this is the real, this is what you must try to understand!'[8] Perhaps they are right, and perhaps the Christian overdoes his emphasis of personality. Anything that we may call 'I' in this world, I venture to think, is very different from the 'imperishable self' and 'spiritual body' of which St. Paul

[7] *Selected Poems from the Dīvāni Shamsi Tabrīz*, ed. R. A. Nicholson, Cambridge, 2nd ed. 1952, pp. 94–7.
[8] Cf. *Chāndogya* Upanishad 8. 7. 1.

speaks, and the first fruit of which is the risen Christ. For the risen Christ was so different from the man Jesus who died on the Cross that even his closest disciples could not at first recognize him. And if such was the nature of the risen Man-God, must we not then too suppose that our own resurrection will have nothing to do with what we here and now call 'I'? And so Teilhard de Chardin says[9]:

The problem of personal survival *per se* doesn't worry me much. Once the fruit of my life is received up into one who is immortal, what can it matter whether I am egotistically conscious of it or have joy of it? I am quite sincere when I say that my personal felicity does not interest me. To be happy it is enough to know that the best of me passes on for ever into one who is more beautiful and greater than I.

This surely is the only true Christian hope both for ourselves and for all the faithful departed. But it is enough; for just as I accept with gratitude all the kindness you have shown me here, because my gratitude and your kindness are both gifts of the Holy Spirit, so must we all accept with gratitude God's greatest gift to all of us who *care*, our physical death. For we have his assurance not only in Christianity but in all the great religions, that what we call death is nothing worse than the breaking up of the husk of our self-love and the release from within it of the sap of a self-less love both human and divine, the Holy Spirit who dwells in the hearts of all.

[9] *Oeuvres* 10, Paris, Editions du Seuil, 1969, pp. 135–6.